AF316693

Shaping A Leader's Soul

For Lasting Impact and Joyful Living

Shaping A Leader's Soul

For Lasting Impact
and Joyful Living

Douglas J. Rumford

Printed and distributed through Lorica Ministries
Copyright © 2025 Douglas J. Rumford

Table of Contents

Introduction

Why Row When You Can Sail?

A small business owner called me while I was writing this manuscript. He was a member of my former congregation, but we hadn't been very close.

"I know this may sound weird," he began, "but I was driving and praying, and your name popped into my head. Don't take this wrong, but I hardly ever think about you."

"No offense taken," I replied. "That makes me even more interested to hear what's on your heart." It surprised me to hear from Joel, and I was curious to hear what he would say.

"I've been praying for someone to talk with about my business," he continued. "The good news is that it is growing like crazy. But I'm struggling to know how to keep Christ at the center of all we do."

Joel described how he had always committed his business to the Lord, "But we need to get back to our core values and core culture," he said. That phone call began a series of ongoing coaching conversations.

Joel isn't alone. Countless leaders in business, education, medicine, law and law enforcement, government, media, the tech sector, sales (and any other sector you can name) want to integrate their faith into their life and work. That's the focus of this book.

I began my ministry in Old Greenwich, Connecticut, just outside of New York City. Most of our congregation's members worked in midtown Manhattan. I confess that initially I struggled with the value of my work compared with their very impressive jobs, titles, and income.

When I dared admit this to a man to whom I'd grown close, he responded with amazement.

"*Are you kidding?*" Glen exclaimed. "I'm just keeping track of the money for our company. You're getting people ready for eternity!"

His good rebuke stopped me in my tracks. And then he went a step further.

"Doug, you also equip us for how to live *now*. Can we get a group of business guys together to meet weekly with you to see how Jesus makes a difference in the business world?"

I jumped at the idea. For more than forty-five years since then, I've met regularly, usually weekly, with groups of leaders (from a variety of contexts in business, education, not-for-profit organizations, and ministry, just to name a few). I called our small groups "D Groups" (D for discipleship). And as you might imagine, I learned more from my fellow disciples than they learned from me. I share many of those lessons in the following pages.

Leaders Are Learners

Good leaders study human character, motivation, drive, and desire. They remain curious. They want to know how to become more effective, efficient, and productive. They observe, they explore. And when leaders face a challenge, they eagerly seek to overcome every obstacle to achieve their goal.

Leaders are success-makers.

Leaders are meaning-makers.

Leaders today face challenges like never before, whether in the form of competitive pressures, political polarization, or accelerating cultural change. Fortunately, the principles of faith and faithful discipleship stand the test of time *and* the chaos of changing circumstances. The key to success lies in applying these principles to changing contexts.

But such success also presents a very big challenge.

What Matters Most?

Many of us have made our whole lives about succeeding. We want to make our lives count and to help make the lives of others count, too. We *don't* want merely to exist. We want to thrive, to flourish, to climb the heights and plumb the depths of life experience.

To accomplish this generally requires the development and pursuit of goals, and there's nothing wrong with having lofty goals. In fact, they're admirable and may be worthy pursuits for you. But in chasing your dream, have you ever felt tempted to compromise some of your core values and relationships?

While ambition and drive have their place, they become liabilities when they eclipse the things that matter most. They can hurt us when they blind us to both tangible and less tangible (but oh-so-important) factors that make life special at the deepest level.

For that reason, many leaders have admitted to reaching a long-desired position or accomplishing a significant goal only to feel a deep-down sense of disappointment. "Something's missing," they say to themselves. "I thought this would finally bring fulfillment, but just where I hoped I would feel whole, I have a hole instead."

We feel this hole whenever (despite all our activity) we neglect whatever matters most. And what matters most? We can think of the answer in several ways.

What's Our Place in the Universe?

We are meaning-makers. We crave reason and purpose.

We are sense-makers. We want things to make sense to our minds and to our hearts.

Ultimate meaning is anchored in the reality beyond us. It's about our place in the universe. Augustine of Hippo—Christian theologian, philosopher, and saint (354–430 AD) — said it this way: "You have made us for yourself, O God, and our hearts are restless until they can find peace in you."[1]

Because we were made by God for God, to find and experience the meaning we crave we must answer three basic questions:

- Where did we come from?
- What has gone wrong with the world?
- What can we do, if anything, to fix it?

Some would add two other questions:

- What is our purpose in life?
- What is our ultimate destiny?

This book will address all these questions, specifically in the context of leaders.

The Illusion of Self-Sufficiency

Life and leadership are hard on the soul. But how often do we increase the difficulty by relying on our own unaided efforts?

Our greatest liability as leaders is the illusion of self-sufficiency. We often succeed because of our faithful, diligent stewardship of God-given abilities, talents, connections, and opportunities. The problem comes when we tend to focus on our efforts and responsibilities and forget that it's not ultimately up to us.

We are wise to remember Jesus' blunt assessment: "Apart from me, you can do nothing" (John 15:5 NIV). Jesus does not say, "Hey, you can accomplish some pretty valuable projects and make some significant contributions when you really work at it. But sometimes you really need me."

The word "nothing" means nothing, as in nothing that truly matters and nothing that will last. None of us are self-sufficient; we are soul-sufficient in Christ. Our ultimate power as followers of Jesus comes from the Holy Spirit living within us. That is why Jesus commands us to abide in Him, to draw our very life from Him as a branch draws its life from the vine.

Or, to use another metaphor, we should pull in our oars and put up a sail.[2]

Sailing, Not Rowing

One way to distinguish between the self-generated life and the soul-energized life is to picture the difference between rowing and sailing. While both are effective means of transportation on water, they have significant differences.

Rowing is entirely self-generated. No effort, no results.

Sailing is wind-generated. The results come from knowing how to harness the wind.

Rowing is best suited to ponds and lakes. It works well in smaller spaces and for simple activities like fishing, but it is extremely difficult and dangerous to try rowing in or against huge ocean waves.

Sailing is best suited for larger bodies of water, where our vessel must move effectively and safely.

A life lived in the power of the Holy Spirit is like pulling in our oars and putting up a sail. The cover of this book features a sailboat at full sail to convey a life of freedom and responsibility. The power to move such a boat comes primarily from the wind, an image for the Holy Spirit. To sail effectively, the boat's pilot must develop the skills and knowledge necessary to harness the wind.

Yes, we have a responsibility for and play an active role in our spiritual development and life work. This concept does not minimize or devalue our responsibility! But it does put first things first.

It's all about our Triune God. We give thanks to God the Father for life; we draw our life from Jesus, who gave His life for us; and we rely on the power of the Holy Spirit, who is God's presence at work in and through us.

So, what is our part? In my earlier book, *SoulShaping (Second Edition)*, I say that "While God makes us and shapes us, God also calls us to join actively in shaping our spiritual lives. Like a wise parent, the Lord cultivates our maturity by not doing all the work for us."[3]

What Is Our Work?

Another way to say "pay attention to the soul" could be "pay attention to the 'inner game.'"[4] For followers of Jesus, the inner game is the realm of the soul. It's the arena where self-awareness, values, and spiritual vitality support and direct the outer game of competence and activity.

Awareness of the inner life fuels and guides our actions. In their book, *Mastering Leadership*, Robert Anderson and William Adams write,

> Competency is only half the game… When we describe great leadership, we describe something beyond skill, capability, and competence… Great leadership is connected with the deepest parts of ourselves. It has more to do with *character, courage,* and *conviction* than it does with specific skills or competencies. Leadership requires *wisdom, self-knowledge,* and *character development* at psychological and spiritual levels. Mastery of leadership requires that we work at these depths and develop mature, conscious awareness.[5]

The elements of this inner game provide the focus of *Shaping A Leader's Soul*. We will mine the depths of the inner processes of self-definition (meaning), motivation, and worldview (mindset). We will determine what defines us, what drives us, and what we value, both in the moment and ultimately.

Three factors are central to shaping a leader's soul. These form the foundation and framework for both developing and sustaining a leader's spiritual health and vitality. This book devotes an entire section to each of these three factors:

Identity: *Start with Who*
Destiny: *Pursue Your Ultimate Purpose*
Partnership: *Link with God's Kingdom Agenda*

Two Types of Books

My editor often says that there are two basic types of books: "About" books and "For" books. "About" books supply information about a subject. They are interesting and can be extremely helpful. They are also relatively easy to write compared to "For" books.

"For" books, by contrast, translate information into life. They take the next step of helping the reader *apply* the information: "If you want this result, do this practice, this exercise, that activity…"

Shaping A Leader's Soul is a "For" book.

I have a passion to bring God's Word to life. I also want to bring to your attention related ideas that will improve how you live. In this book, I want to do both in a comprehensive way that includes your mind, heart, and behavior in your daily life as a leader. What will this entail? With God's help…

You will renew your mind.

You will identify clearly and concisely what matters most to spiritual leaders. You will understand the biblical basis for your identity in Christ. Your clear sense of identity will provide an unshakable foundation that keeps you spiritually grounded despite the wonderful rewards, alluring temptations, and devastating heartaches and disappointments that are part and parcel of leadership. You will also come to know the spiritual principles, processes, and practices for developing and sustaining vitality in spiritual leadership.

You will awaken your heart.

You will gain a growing self-knowledge of your spiritual condition, personal vulnerabilities and liabilities, as well as your passions and dreams in Christ. You will develop the desire and determination to practice the most appropriate spiritual exercises that generate vitality, joy, and power for your daily life and leadership responsibilities. You will experience an increased excitement for living in the power of the Holy Spirit as the Lord transforms you "from one degree of glory to another" (2 Corinthians 3:18 NRSVue). You will increase your hope in the power of the spiritual disciplines to change and shape lives.

You will live and lead differently.

You will become increasingly proficient in living with spiritual energy and sensitivity, experiencing Christ's abundant life moment by moment in both life and work. You will develop and practice a consistent plan of soul care that energizes your daily routines. You will be equipped to create a culture of spiritual vitality by leading people and projects so that all involved understand and practice the appropriate principles of spiritual leadership for their own spiritual well-being and effectiveness. You will live so that your personal faith increasingly shapes you to act and to lead in congruence with your core beliefs and values.

Interact with the Ideas

You will get the most from this book if you actively engage with it as you read. If you're anything like me, you often carry on an inner dialog with an author—evaluating, affirming, questioning, even rejecting the ideas you read. But that dialog is usually like writing on the sand, gone as soon as the tide of everyday life breaks on the shore of daily responsibility.

How many helpful insights are lost? How much useful wisdom evaporates like a dream upon awakening? Leaders who want to grow will pay attention to the input they receive and to the inner dialogue they experience.

So, I urge you, don't merely skim this book. Sink into the ideas, thoughts, images, concepts, principles, and Scriptures presented.

As you read, interact with the ideas presented. You may want to read the entire book first, for an overview. Then read it again more slowly, like a letter you've discovered from a dear friend or relative.

Give Journaling a Try!

C. S. Lewis said, "Whenever you are fed up with life, start writing. Ink is the great cure for all human ills, as I have found long ago."[6]

Get the *Shaping A Leader's Soul Workbook* designed to accompany this book, or get a blank notebook, and start to record your thoughts and reflections as you read. Start with writing one sentence! You may copy a single thought, phrase or sentence from what you've read and that's all. Eventually, jot down *why* that thought captured your attention, why you agree or disagree, or a related concept it brought to mind. In time, you will begin to walk the fascinating landscape of your own heart, mind, and soul—a wonderland as varied as the geography of our planet. You'll be surprised how the act of writing moves an idea deeper into your heart and life.

Sail On!

Too many of us live the self-reliant, self-generated life of rowing. And rowing definitely works...for a while. At some point, however, it utterly and inescapably fails, even as it limits our full potential.

Jesus offers us a better way, the Spirit-empowered life of sailing.

This book invites you to discover the power and joy of God's wind, the Holy Spirit. It encourages you to tap the energy of the Holy Spirit working in *you*.

Let's pull in our oars and put up the sail!

Part One

What's Soul Got to Do with It?

What good is it for someone to gain the whole world,
and yet lose or forfeit their very self?

—JESUS IN LUKE 9:25 (NIV)

Ambition and drive have their place. They make life exciting and fulfilling and can bring many benefits. But they also can become liabilities when they eclipse the things that matter most, blinding us to the intangible-but-oh-so-important factors that make life special at the deepest level.

Jesus teaches clearly that soul plays the *essential* role for a leader's lasting impact and joyful living. When we ignore the soul, moral failure destroys great achievements. When we neglect the soul, our corrupted moral inclination misuses great abilities. When we forget the soul, we waste tremendous resources on projects and programs that bear no lasting fruit.

Soul is not an added ingredient; it is essential.

"The common cognomen of this world among the misguided and superstitious is a 'vale (valley) of tears'… Call the world if you please 'The vale of soul-making,' then you will find out the use of the world."

—JOHN KEATS, BRITISH POET (1795-1821)[7]

Let it once be fixed that a person's ambition is to fit into God's plan for him and he has a north star ever in sight to guide him steadily over any sea, however shoreless it seems. He has a compass that points true in the thickest fog and fiercest storm, and regardless of magnetic rocks.

—S.D. GORDON[8]

Your Majesty,
Some men's ambition is art,
Some men's ambition is fame
Some men's ambition is gold,
My ambition is the souls of men.

—SALVATION ARMY GENERAL WILLIAM BOOTH
TO KING EDWARD VII (1904)

01
Going for the Gold

The 1993 movie *Cool Runnings* is loosely based on the true story of the debut of the Jamaica national bobsled team (yes, you read that correctly—as in Jamaica, the Caribbean nation!) which competed in the 1988 Winter Olympics in Calgary, Alberta, Canada.

In the story, Derice Bannock, a top 100-meter runner, failed to qualify at the Olympic trial for the 1988 Summer Olympics. But since he refused to give up on his dream of competing in the Olympics, he made the unlikely choice of developing a bobsled team to compete on behalf of his Caribbean nation.

Derice and his best friend, Sanka Coffie, a champion pushcart racer, sought out Irv Blitzer (played by John Candy), an American bobsled competitor and two-time Gold Medalist at the 1968 Winter Olympics. Irv finished first in two events again during the 1972 Winter Olympics but was later disqualified for cheating. Irv retired in disgrace to Jamaica, where he led an impoverished life as a bookie.

Derice's persistence eventually convinced the very reluctant Irv to be their coach and return to the Olympic life he left behind. In a pivotal scene, Derice dared to ask Irv why he cheated.

"It's quite simple, really," Irv responded. "I *had* to win. You see, Derice, I'd made winning my whole life. And when you make winning your whole life, you have to keep on winning—no matter what. Do you understand that?"

"No, I don't understand, coach," responded Derice, "I don't. You had two gold medals. You had it all."

"Derice, a gold medal is a wonderful thing; but if you're not enough without it, you'll never be enough with it."[9]

What's *your* gold medal? Take a few moments to name the achievements you value most. They may be things like:

- gaining financial independence
- writing a bestseller
- being part of a top sales team

- starting your own company
- joining the medical team of a nationally recognized healthcare center
- becoming an actor
- playing first chair with a renowned orchestra
- inventing a life-improving product

While you may not resort to cheating to obtain your own "gold medal," do you ever feel tempted to compromise any of your core values and relationships to chase your dream? We will pay a heavy price if we chase success at the expense of:

- our primary relationships
- our family
- our self-care
- our spiritual health
- our God-given call
- our relationship with God

Too often it takes a dramatic loss or threat to break us from the "gold-spell" that entrances and drives us. Maybe it's a frightening medical report, or a child's hostility and rebellion, or a partner's threat of divorce or separation, or a termination. Or it could be something else entirely.

Whatever it is, we don't have to wait for a crisis. Could that be why you're taking time to read this now? You want to better understand life and abundant living. More than that, you want to *experience* this kind of thoughtful, abundant life.

The good news is you can.

02
Something's Missing

Author Arthur C. Brooks coined the term, "The Striver's Curse," in his book *From Strength to Strength*. He used it to describe people who strive to be excellent at what they do but who often wind up in a terrifying inevitable decline, their successes increasingly unsatisfying, and their relationships lacking.[10]

Brooks made this observation on his fortieth birthday, having met or exceeded all his goals. "I had gotten my heart's desire," he wrote, "at least as I imagined it, but it didn't bring the joy I envisioned."[11]

It's not hard to see Brooks' candid admission echoed in countless other lives.

Achieving a goal, even a lifelong goal, often does not lead to lasting joy. As playwright George Bernard Shaw wrote, "There are two sources of unhappiness in life. One is not getting what you want; the other is getting it."[12]

When we look at the outward success of major cultural icons, we typically get the wrong idea of what that success means to those who achieved it. In their signature song, "I Can't Get No (Satisfaction)," the Rolling Stones gave raw expression to this visceral discontent and frustration. Mick Jagger later said about this track, "'Satisfaction' was my view of the world, my frustration with everything… (and disgust with) America, its advertising syndrome, the constant barrage."[13]

Have you arrived at some desired position or achieved a long-sought goal, only to find something missing? Or perhaps that discovery lies yet ahead.

In his book *Half Time*, Bob Buford describes the shift he finally made from success to significance:

> During the first half of your life, if you are like me, you probably did not have time to think about how you would spend the rest of your life. You probably rushed through college, fell in love, married, embarked on a career, climbed upward, and acquired many things to help make the journey comfortable…. But now

you yearn for something more than success… you want to make sure that you finish well, that you leave something behind no one can take away from you. If the first half was a quest for success, the second half is a journey to significance.[14]

It's important to realize that this shift need not manifest itself as a career change or as a resignation from a successful career. The point is to grasp the revised mindset that defines how we view ourselves and how we do everything (more on this later in Part Four).

For now, it's enough to remember the wisdom offered by the adage: "If you keep doing what you're doing, you'll keep getting what you've got." Do you *want* to keep getting what you've got? If you answer "no," then how do you get off the hamster wheel?

03
What's Missing?

We have a sense that something is missing. But what is it? We'll see that an earth-bound, time-bound search for satisfaction ultimately comes up empty. Where else can we look?

Albert Einstein, the rigorous, creative physicist, intrigues us when he says that what's missing too often in our lives is a sense of the "mystical:"

> The most beautiful and profound emotion we can experience is the sensation of the mystical. It is the sower of all true science. He to whom this emotion is a stranger, who can no longer wonder and stand rapt in awe, is as good as dead.[15]

Einstein suggested that something more exists that lies beyond the experience of our five senses of taste, touch, smell, hearing, and seeing. Something more is out there for us than scientific materialism. A realm of reality, both beyond and woven into human experience, beckons us.

Einstein worked for many years at the Institute for Advanced Studies on the campus of Princeton University, a school founded for the training of Christian ministers. Dartmouth College, another Ivy League school, also was founded to train young people for Christian ministry and to show students how to relate God to all learning. Though in time Dartmouth, like Princeton, drifted from its spiritual purpose, the importance of the spiritual asserted itself when seven of its students were asphyxiated one night in the dormitories by the fumes of a faulty furnace. At their funeral service, Ernest Martin Hopkins, president of Dartmouth from 1916 to 1945, said:

> At a time like this the college is most effectively sheared of its affectation, its petty pose, and its specious sophistries. We see life in its great dimensions rather than subjectively…we begin to sense that rationalism is not all, and that there is no harder or colder form of materialism than the materialism of pure intellect not tempered by the influence of heart and soul. We begin to

understand assertions like that of Aubry L. Moore, the brilliant young English essayist, that human nature claims to be both rational and religious and the life that is not both is neither.[16]

Ironically, the sources of satisfaction we pursue often leave us more dissatisfied. "Our attachments are like drinking salt water," goes an old saying. "We think we will cure our thirst, and instead it drives us mad with thirst."[17]

French mathematician Blaise Pascal gave us yet another classic explanation for the emptiness we often feel: "There is a God-shaped vacuum in the heart of each man that cannot be satisfied by any created thing but only by God the Creator, made known through Jesus Christ." I was fascinated to discover that this quote is a paraphrase derived from a passage in *Pensées*, a collection of Pascal's fragmentary thoughts published posthumously in 1670, where Pascal actually wrote that "this infinite abyss can be filled only with an infinite and immutable object; in other words, by God himself."[18]

The Problem of Incomplete Joy

Alexis de Tocqueville, a French political thinker and historian best known for his books *Democracy in America* (appearing in two volumes, in 1835 and 1840), analyzed the rising living standards and social conditions of individuals in Western societies and their relationship to the market and state.

"America is great," he wrote, "because she is good. If America ceases to be good, America will cease to be great." He also declared, "Liberty cannot be established without morality, nor morality without faith."

De Tocqueville also noted that although Americans believed prosperity could bring deep happiness, any such a hope was an illusion. Why? Because "the incomplete joys of this world will never satisfy [the human] heart." He saw this played out in a "strange melancholy often haunting inhabitants of democracies in the midst of abundance." This melancholy, of course, followed the bitter fruit of idolatry that *always* leads to disappointment. False gods never give us what they promise.[19]

The Problem of Shallow Thinking

Human beings crave both a reason *and* a passion for their existence. We want things to make sense to our minds and to our hearts. We want to know our place in the universe.

We derive meaning from our understanding of the world and how it works. The framework for meaning is typically called our worldview. Our quest for meaning must respond to several essential questions:

> Our major task in life is to discover what is true and to live in step with that truth…. Every worldview can be analyzed by the way it answers three basic questions: Where did we come from, and who are we (creation)? What has gone wrong with the world (fall)? And what can we do to fix it (redemption)? These three questions form a grid that we can use to break down the inner logic of every belief system or philosophy.[20]

Some would also add the questions:

- What is our purpose in life (strongly linked to our creation identity)?
- And what is our ultimate destiny? Is it limited to this earthly life, or does some kind of existence follow this earthly life?

Those who have no response to these questions find themselves tossed to and fro' by life's circumstances. They fall victim to passing fads and philosophies. When you take the time to answer these questions and figure out what you believe and why you believe it, you move from a shallow, wave-tossed life to a deeply anchored life.

The Danger of "Success"

Jesus gives us several sobering warnings about the dangers of "success." He asks, "What do you benefit if you gain the whole world but are yourself lost or destroyed?" (Luke 9:25, NLT). The Amplified Version renders this verse, "For what does it profit a man if he gains the whole world [wealth, fame, success], and loses or forfeits himself?" Either way, we see that worldly success can endanger our eternal well-being.

Jesus' message is so important that he framed this principle in what we commonly call The Parable of the Rich Fool:

> Then He told them a parable, saying, "There was a rich man whose land was very fertile and productive. And he began thinking to himself, 'What shall I do, since I have no place [large enough in which] to store my crops?' Then he said, 'This is what I will do: I will tear down my storehouses and build larger ones, and I will store all my grain and my goods there.

And I will say to my soul, "Soul, you have many good things stored up, [enough] for many years; rest and relax, eat, drink and be merry (celebrate continually).'" But God said to him, 'You fool! This very night your soul is required of you; and now who will own all the things you have prepared?' So it is for the one who continues to store up and hoard possessions for himself and is not rich [in his relationship] toward God." (Luke 12:16-21, AMP)

Something exists that's far more important than material wealth and security.

04
You Gotta Have Soul

Most of us frame leadership in terms of power, position, competencies, and personal characteristics. When we ask if leaders are born or cultivated, the common questions center on "nature" verses "nurture." What roles do personality and temperament play? What roles do instruction and training play?

But few ask, "What role does the soul play?"

Jesus teaches that soul plays the *essential* role in a leader's lasting impact. When we ignore the soul, great achievements crumble, often through moral failure. When we neglect the soul, we misdirect great abilities through a corrupted moral inclination. When we forget the soul, we waste tremendous resources on projects and programs that bear no lasting fruit.

Soul is not merely an added ingredient; it is indispensable.

Soul is not like a room added to a building; soul is the building.

Soul is not optional; it is essential.

Soul is not "unworldly;" soul is the real world.

What Is the Soul?

The soul is the essence of our humanity; that's my working definition.[21] The soul is the primary seat of the *Imago Dei* (Latin for "the image of God") that characterized humanity from the moment of creation, as stated in Genesis 1:26-28:

> Then God said, "Let us make humans in our image, according to our likeness, and let them have dominion over the fish of the sea and over the birds of the air and over the cattle and over all the wild animals of the earth and over every creeping thing that creeps upon the earth."
>
> So God created humans in his image,
> in the image of God he created them;
> male and female he created them.

God blessed them, and God said to them, "Be fruitful and multiply and fill the earth and subdue it and have dominion over the fish of the sea and over the birds of the air and over every living thing that moves upon the earth" (Genesis 1:26-28, NRSVue).

The Message paraphrase of these verses sees being in God's image as "reflecting" God's nature. We see this reflection especially in our communion with God and receiving from Him the responsibility for the governance and stewardship of creation.

The soul is the life-force inherent in breath. The biblical concept of soul comes from the Hebrew word for "breath" (*ruach*) in Genesis 2:7:

… then the Lord God formed man from the dust of the ground and breathed into his nostrils the breath of life, and the man became a living being. (NRSVue).

Dallas Willard described the word "soul" like this:

"Soul" is here defined as the hidden or "spiritual" side of the person. It includes an individual's thoughts and feelings, along with heart or will, with its intents and choices. It also includes an individual's bodily life and social relations, which, in their inner meaning and nature, are just as "hidden" as the thoughts and feelings. The secret to a strong, healthy, and fruitful ministerial life lies in how we work with God in all these dimensions. Together they make up the real person.[22]

Willard presents a diagram of concentric circles in which the outmost circle is the soul. Moving inward, the circles are "Social," "Body," "Mind," and "Spirit." While we may instinctively assume the soul is the innermost circle, I agree with Willard that the soul encompasses our complete human experience. The soul, then, as the outmost circle embraces and includes every aspect of our humanity.

The soul is the connecting point of your inner life. The soul is the means by which you connect with the Lord and your eternal destiny. The soul is the operational center for your mind, body, will, and emotions. It's the control room.

We could compare the soul to a computer's Operating System (OS), the software that controls and supports a computer's basic functions, such as scheduling tasks, executing programs and applications, and controlling peripherals. The OS makes everything work and function together. When it works properly, the OS is "invisible," operating in the background. A malfunction in the OS negatively affects everything else. Small bugs may cause little disruption, while big problems can cause a crash.

Let's extend the metaphor a bit. Let's call the soul the "heartware" of a life, its spiritual operating system. That heartware runs a life, whether it is polluted by sin or redeemed by grace.

The soul is the space (but not a localized place) where all our life programs meet. The soul is our inner life, that feature or element of our human nature that embraces our essence, our personhood, and our personality. It's the core that guides our thinking, feeling, motivation, and actions. It is the locus of spiritual connection with others, with the external world, and with spiritual existence.

The soul concerns itself with life's deepest issues, among them:

- *Morality*: What's right and wrong?
- *Values*: What's important?
- *Desires*: What do I want?
- *Motivation*: What gets me going?
- *Blocks*: What holds me back?
- *Meaning*: How do I make sense of my life?

But let's not push the metaphor too far! We are not pre-programmed machines. We are organic, living, breathing beings. Even in our life of faith in Christ, we are subject to the highest and lowest of human desires and behaviors.

How do we thrive as human beings? We thrive when we take care of our souls and intentionally nurture our inner lives.

05

A Metaphor for Satisfaction, Significance, and Joy

While none of us is self-sufficient, all of us who are in Christ are soul-sufficient. The apostle John said it like this:

> You, dear children, are from God and have overcome them, because the one who is in you is greater than the one who is in the world (1 John 4:4, NIV).

The apostle Paul put it this way:

> Now to him who is able to do immeasurably more than all we ask or imagine, according to his power that is at work within us, to him be glory in the church and in Christ Jesus throughout all generations, for ever and ever! Amen (Ephesians 3:20-21, NIV).

Jesus himself commands us to draw our very life from Him as a branch draws its life from the vine:

> Abide in me as I abide in you. Just as the branch cannot bear fruit by itself unless it abides in the vine, neither can you unless you abide in me. I am the vine; you are the branches. Those who abide in me and I in them bear much fruit, because apart from me you can do nothing (John 15:4-5, NRSVue).

Abiding in Jesus is not an option, as He made clear by his next statement:

> Whoever does not abide in me is thrown away like a branch and withers; such branches are gathered, thrown into the fire, and burned (John 15:6, NRSVue).

Missionary C. T. Studd (1860-1931) considered all these biblical truths and wrote the famous couplet:

> Only one life, 'twill soon be past,
> Only what's done for Christ will last.

A great danger for leaders is depending on their own effort to pursue projects that won't last. I think we all know times when we have strained to make something work—only to see it fail miserably. Early in my ministry, I suggested the idea of reorganizing our congregation's leadership structure. The appropriate motions were passed, the appropriate committee was formed, the necessary conversations were held, and a thoughtful proposal was developed. It was all done "decently and in order,"[23] and it fell absolutely flat. I put in a great deal of time and energy that didn't advance the kingdom-focus of the church's leadership.

As mentioned in the introduction, one way to envision the self-sufficient, self-generated life is rowing. I was rowing upstream against the culture and priorities of my congregation when I focused on leadership structure. The result, in addition to my personal discouragement, was a modest erosion of trust and confidence in my leadership.

Rowing is one aspect of what Jesus meant by building on the sand (see Matthew 7:26-27). Leaders need to discern when projects express their personal vanity and ambition rather than genuine contributions to the welfare of their team, organization, and clients.

In contrast, the soul-dependent, soul-energized life is like sailing. There's nothing like the energizing feeling of cutting across an open ocean with a stiff breeze moving your boat swiftly toward your desired destination! By God's grace, I've experienced times when God filled the sails of an idea and accomplished more than we could have asked or imagined. The COVID-19 pandemic was one of the most challenging seasons churches have faced in this generation. Our congregation, like the vast majority in the confusion and restrictions of the early days of the crisis, shifted to an online format. But we were quickly confronted with the fact that the men and women in our emerging ministry to the homeless had no place to watch our services. "What about us?" they asked.

So, Patrick, one of our members, drove his SUV into our church parking lot and set up a TV monitor for the homeless women and men to watch outside. Soon other members began to gather outside, longing for community. Over time, the people committed to watching the sermon also wanted "live music," so some of our musicians and worship leaders joined "parking lot church." Eventually, that group moved into neighborhoods surrounding our campus, meeting in cul-de-sacs. They asked their neighbors' permission to meet on Sunday mornings; and more often than not, those neighbors attended the services. Unintentionally, "Street Church" became a missional strategy for evangelism and growth in a time when most congregations saw decline.

That's sailing! People caught a vision and engaged with energy. We didn't recruit people to adopt some idea we had. We didn't do surveys or develop detailed plans. Our members simply climbed on board and got excited about it. It became one of the most exciting times in recent memory. "Now all glory to God, who is able, through his mighty power at work within us, to accomplish infinitely more than we might ask or think" (Ephesians 3:20, NLT).

06
From Compartmentalization to Integration

Too often we view our lives in segments rather than as an integrated soul. We have our work life, our family life, our personal life, our relationships, our spiritual life, our community life, our church life, our financial life, our service to others, and our recreational life. All separate.

We feel pushed and pulled by the demands and opportunities in each area. We do our best to achieve a life/work balance but always fall short because we have an unworkable model based on fragmentation and compartmentalization rather than on integration and wholeness.

Faith offers us the way to integration. The Gospel account of Mary and Martha illustrates what I call the "Fit or Form" challenge.[24] Jesus' encounter with Mary and Martha illustrates this choice between two distinct approaches to life:

> As Jesus and the disciples continued on their way to Jerusalem, they came to a certain village where a woman named Martha welcomed him into her home. Her sister, Mary, sat at the Lord's feet, listening to what he taught. But Martha was distracted by the big dinner she was preparing. She came to Jesus and said, "Lord, doesn't it seem unfair to you that my sister just sits here while I do all the work? Tell her to come and help me."
>
> But the Lord said to her, "My dear Martha, you are worried and upset over all these details! There is only one thing worth being concerned about. Mary has discovered it, and it will not be taken away from her." (Luke 10:38-42, NLT)

Martha felt distracted, anxious, and troubled about many things, while Mary sat at Jesus' feet as He taught. When Martha complained about Mary's lack of help, Jesus told her that although she felt worried and upset about many things, at *that moment* only one thing was needed. Her sister had chosen the better way and the Lord refused to take it away from her.

Martha tried to fit Christ into her already-full life, while Mary formed her life around Christ, choosing the "one necessary thing." Jesus didn't mean that preparing dinner and making a home suitable for guests were unimportant, but only that at that moment a much more important thing was happening. Getting food ready and cleaning up the house could wait until after the Messiah, the Lord of Glory, had finished filling up the souls of His hearers.

The Mary approach views every aspect of life in terms of faith and faithfulness. A starting point for this approach in our own experience is to frame our life and work around the great commandments. Recall Jesus' teaching in Matthew 22:

> But when the Pharisees heard that he had silenced the Sadducees, they gathered together. And one of them, a lawyer, asked him a question to test him. "Teacher, which is the great commandment in the Law?" And he said to him, "You shall love the Lord your God with all your heart and with all your soul and with all your mind. This is the great and first commandment. And a second is like it: You shall love your neighbor as yourself. On these two commandments depend all the Law and the Prophets" (Matthew 22:34-40, ESV).

We can develop this approach with some basic questions, such as:

How do I show you my love, Lord, in the workplace?
How do I love my neighbor by the way I do my work?
How am I loving myself in all that I do?

We make the mistake of viewing our lives in segments. What happens when we view everything in terms of loving God, our neighbor, and ourselves? In that case, everything takes on a different tone, a different aspect, a different dimension. Instead of telling ourselves, "I have to balance my bank account," we say, "Thank you, Lord, for providing for my needs. Fill me with your spirit now as I steward these resources."

Instead of telling ourselves, "I have to go this meeting," we tell ourselves, "I'm going to use this meeting as an opportunity to show my colleagues I care about them. I may not say that in words, but my respectful listening, my words of affirmation, my patience, my willingness to participate will be expressions of God's love shown in practical ways."

Instead of telling ourselves, "I'm just gonna veg-out and watch videos," we tell ourselves, "Lord, help me rest and recharge myself the best way possible."

With a bit of effort, you can reframe everything in terms of the great commandments. That effort brings your soul to life—and brings soul-life to all you do.

07

The Inner Game Runs the Outer Game

In his classic book *The Inner Game of Tennis*, author W. Timothy Gallway wrote:

> It is the thesis of this book that neither mastery nor satisfaction can be found in the playing of any game without giving some attention to the relatively neglected skills of the inner game.[25]

Christian leaders will find it helpful to compare paying attention to the soul to paying attention to the "inner game"[26] of self-awareness, values, and spiritual vitality. Paying attention to the inner game of purpose and priorities directs our outer game of competence and activity. The inner processes of self-definition, motivation, and worldview define us, drive us, and provide for us what we value most, both in the moment and ultimately.

But how do we access that inner game? Scripture gives us countless avenues. Read and reflect on the principles expressed in each of these:

> Thou dost keep him in perfect peace,
> *whose mind is stayed on thee,*
> because he trusts in thee (Isaiah 26:3, RSV, emphasis added).

> Finally, brothers and sisters, whatever is true, whatever is noble, whatever is right, whatever is pure, whatever is lovely, whatever is admirable—if anything is excellent or praiseworthy—*think about such things.* Whatever you have learned or received or heard from me or seen in me—put it into practice. And the God of peace will be with you (Philippians 4:8-9, NRSVue, emphasis added).

> For this reason, *I kneel before the Father,* from whom every family in heaven and on earth derives its name. I pray that out of his glorious riches he may strengthen you with power through his Spirit in your inner being, so that Christ may dwell in your hearts through faith (Ephesians 3:14-17, NIV, emphasis added).

I urge you, brothers and sisters, in view of God's mercy, to offer
your bodies as a living sacrifice, holy and pleasing to God—
this is your true and proper worship. Do not conform to the
pattern of this world but be *transformed by the renewing of your
mind*. Then you will be able to test and approve what God's will
is—his good, pleasing and perfect will (Romans 12:1-2, NIV,
emphasis added).

Scripture also calls us to resist distractions and attend to our
inner lives as a top priority. Here are multiples translations of a key
exhortation:

Guard your heart above all else,
for it determines the course of your life (Proverbs 4:23, NLT).

Above all else, guard your heart,
for everything you do flows from it (Proverbs 4:23, NIV).

Keep vigilant watch over your heart;
that's where life starts (Proverbs 4:23, *The Message*).

In the Bible, the word "heart" most commonly denotes the mind,
but it can also include our emotions, our will, and our whole inner
being.[27] To "guard" means to keep watch over, to protect against
attack, to shield from harmful influences. We protect ourselves from
spiritual weakness by cultivating spiritual health.

We nurture the inner game by paying attention to our mind, our
heart, our will, and our emotions. It's unhealthy to ignore our feelings
and to suppress our personal concerns. It's not a waste of time to pray
and spend time in God's Word! Leaders are like finely tuned instruments that get pummeled by the stress and strain of life. They require
time for re-tuning, for re-calibrating.

I had the privilege of going backstage to be with Bernie Leadon,
one of the lead guitarists with the Eagles (the rock group known for
"Take It Easy," "Peaceful Easy Feeling," and "Witchy Woman") when
they came to the Forum in Los Angeles during a national tour. My
friend, Bill (a friend of Bernie), got three VIP tickets and backstage
passes so he could bring my wife Sarah and me to the concert. As a
guitarist myself, I felt eager to meet Bernie and get a look backstage.
Bernie took us from his green room to see his two racks of guitars
set up below the stage. Twelve guitars! I knew that each guitar had a
unique sound. "They're all fun, and I like to play them all, but most

important," Bernie said in response to my admiration of his instruments, "I need to be sure the guitar is in tune. That's why I tune or change guitars after nearly every song."

Be sure you're in tune. That will preach! We need to tune at the start of the day but also to re-tune throughout the day. That's the purpose of the inner game. It reminds us who we are and whose we are. Above all, we stay tuned to the Lord.

In other words, we learn to move with comfort and agility in the realm of the Spirit.

08
Spiritual Disciplines Keep Your Inner Game Alive

While it may not seem natural at first to "move with comfort and agility in the realm of the Spirit," the Lord and God's people throughout the centuries have provided practical tools to help us shape our souls, so that we can enjoy effective and satisfying lives.

Just as physical exercises are tailored for cardio workouts, strength training, flexibility and mobility, so too are exercises for the soul tailored for our soul's varied needs. Too often we neglect the inner world or allow it to get eclipsed by the immediate demands and clamoring voices of the outside world.

Spiritual health reflects and impacts *every* area of life, from how we spend our time to how we manage our finances. It affects and is affected by how we live in our primary relationships and how we treat our neighbors. It's visible in how we think, feel, and act.

In *SoulShaping (Second Edition)*, I presented five vital signs of spiritual health. Each vital sign is supported by a cluster of three disciplines.

God's *pace* redeems your time.

- Redeem Your Time
- Enjoy Sabbath Rest
- Celebrate Sacred Milestones

God's *presence* fills your heart.

- Preview
- Review
- Prayer

God's *perspective* renews your mind.

- Bible Study
- Meditation
- Spiritual Input

God's *power* strengthens your will.

- Fasting
- Silence
- Solitude

God's *purpose* directs your steps.
- Character
- Community
- Calling

Later in this book I will explain these more fully and suggest specific spiritual disciplines for each factor involved in shaping a leader's soul. These disciplines provide practical steps to shift our focus from the outward pressures to the inner springs of life. They help us recalibrate our priorities, reaffirm our values, and recenter our scattered energy.

09
Sink, Don't Skim

The subtitle of this book, *For Lasting Impact and Joyful Living*, highlights the rewards for developing and sustaining a soul-focused concept of leadership that is as broad as life's responsibilities and as deep as life's ultimate reality. And it celebrates the one consistent element of a leader's life: the soul.

It also identifies the dual purpose of leaders in both serving others effectively in a meaningful way (significance) and in experiencing the goodness and pleasure of work well done (satisfaction). Lasting impact and joyful living—both are great treasures.

What other words in English often pair up with "treasure"? I think of terms such as "hidden," "lost," and "buried." The truth is that you don't usually find treasure just by skimming the surface. You must dig, explore, and plunge into the depths. That's also a key strategy for personal growth.

When you actively engage with the concepts in this book, you're really searching for buried treasure. You'll be interacting with gems that God wants to use to enrich your life and reveal to you a clearer, more detailed picture of you.

I think Professor Adam Neder has good advice for readers. He would counsel you to *let* this book read you:

> The very best books are reading you. They expose and illuminate you, cut through your ignorance and self-deception, challenge your misconceptions, and reveal you to yourself. We read because we are not yet who we want to be.[28]

Use this material to help you sink more deeply into your own thoughts about leadership and your personal journey, values, obstacles, and hopes. While I heartily affirm (and provide) life and leadership coaching and spiritual direction, the ultimate goal of every effective coach and spiritual director is to equip people to do a significant amount of self-coaching.

I encourage you to engage deeply with the rest of the content in this book. As you do, I believe you will be greatly inspired and enriched, especially as you journal about your thoughts! I urge you to revisit them periodically as you chew on this material.

Sail on!

Part Two

Identity:
Start with Who

The middle three parts of this book are based on in-depth reflection over Jesus' final moments with His disciples before His betrayal, crucifixion, and resurrection—in other words, at the culmination of our Lord's earthly mission. They are specifically patterned on three leadership insights revealed in John 13, each of which are central to shaping a leader's soul. These three concepts form the foundation and framework for both developing and sustaining a leader's spiritual health and vitality.

Part Two, Identity, insists that we start with Who:

Jesus, knowing that the Father had given all things into His hands, and that He had come from God . . .

—JOHN 13:3 (NKJV)

Our identity forms the bedrock of our lives and gives life meaning. Leaders who truly know who they are in Christ and how they relate to the Creator of the universe will have a robust sense of worth that fuels a holy self-confidence. Identity is the essence of their perception of reality, the framework for their motivation (their "Why"), the foundation for their sense and source of purpose, and the basis for measuring of success.

*…the Holy Spirit descended on Jesus in bodily form like a dove.
And a voice came from heaven: "You are my Son, whom I love;
with you I am well pleased."*

—LUKE 3:22 (NIV ALT)

*The devil said to Jesus,
"**If** you are the Son of God, tell this stone to become bread."
Jesus answered, "It is written: 'Man shall not live on bread alone.'"*

—LUKE 4:3-4 (NIV, EMPHASIS ADDED)

*The devil led Jesus to Jerusalem and had him stand on
the highest point of the temple. "**If** you are the Son of God,"
he said, "throw yourself down from here…"*

Jesus answered, "It is said: 'Do not put the Lord your God to the test.'"

—LUKE 4:9, 12 (NIV, EMPHASIS ADDED)

*I am not the esteem, I can collect through competition,
but the love I have freely received from God.*

—HENRI NOUWEN[29]

*There are no ordinary people. You have never talked to a mere
mortal. Nations, cultures, arts, civilization—these are mortal, and
their life is to ours as the life of a gnat. But it is immortals whom we
joke with, work with, marry, snub, and exploit—immortal horrors
or everlasting splendors.*

— C. S. LEWIS[30]

10
What's Your Real Name?

In their Gold Medallion Award-winning books, *Tales of the Kingdom* and *Tales of the Resistance*, Karen and David Mains tell of an orphan boy from the wicked Enchanted City, scarred by the evil practice of branding.

Scarboy, as he was known, escaped the Enchanted City and entered the Great Park, a place of goodness and healing. In that place, he was adopted and given a new name, Hero. Eventually, the time came for Hero to return to the Enchanted City to help overthrow the Enchanter.

One day, Hero saw the Good King, the true ruler of the city, challenge the evil Enchanter (the fire wizard) for the right to restore his kingdom. But then, inexplicably, Hero watched the King drive away, leaving Hero exposed. Let's pick up the narrative:

Suddenly he knew he was standing alone in the presence of the Enchanter in the bone cold night air. He quickly covered his cheek with his hand, pulled his collar up around his neck, and started to creep away.

"Scarboy!"

Too late.

"Scarboy!"

Hero stopped. He waited for a cudgel blow to the head, a burning poker in his back. He expected the death drums to paralyze his soul, the song of the Naysayers to strike terror in his heart—but the strange silence continued, except for the old name, spoken by the old enemy.

Hero refused to turn around and look at the fire wizard. One look and he would be under the power of his evil eye. Did he have any power himself? Fool! How could one lad withstand the Enchanter?…

"Scarboy!" The ugly voice called again.

Again, Hero refused to turn around…Then he heard it. The sound rose unbidden from some distant place, the one-note sound of the Rite of Adoption; flutelike, faint, faraway. H-m-m-m-m-m-m-m, it began. One lonely sound.

"SCARBOY!" the Enchanter shrieked, calling the old name frantically, as though he sensed power diminishing.

Little time; soon the silence would be broken. The one note hum swelled, filling his heart, beating wildly beneath his breastbone, gladdening his ear.

That was it! He might be scarred, but he was Scarboy no longer. He didn't belong here, in this evil place, this city doomed by enchantment. His home was Great Park, the King's place. His people were the people of Great Park—Mercie and Caretaker were his true parents.[31]

Hero's new identity freed him from the bondage of his scars—and from the power of the wizard. He was no longer controlled by the forces of darkness but was set free to walk in the light.

That's the power of an internally grounded identity.

When Jesus first met Andrew's brother, He said, "You are Simon the son of John. You shall be called Cephas" (which means Peter) (John 1:42 ESV). When Jesus renamed Simon with the nickname "Peter," He showed us that He both understands our weakness and has the power to transform us. Jesus revealed that He sees us not merely in terms of what we are, but also what we can become by the power of God. Even as parents name their children, so Jesus' renaming of Peter also asserted His authority over Peter and gave us another glimpse of His call to be born again. That's why identity is our starting point.

Who are you?

And who tells you who you are?

When you resolve these questions, everything begins to align.

11
Start with Who Before Why

The marvel and the mystery of the Christian life is that we, by faith, are born again, becoming new creations in Christ. We receive a new self, a new identity, which depends not on what we can achieve but on what we are willing to receive.

This means that anyone who belongs to Christ has become a new person. The old life is gone; a new life has begun (2 Corinthians 5:17, NLT)!

There's power in knowing who you are. Power to break old bonds and avoid new ones. Power to know your true home, your true community, your true purpose. As in the account of Hero that we read earlier:

That was it! He might be scarred, but he was Scarboy no longer. He didn't belong here, in this evil place, this city doomed by enchantment. His home was Great Park, the King's place. His people were the people of Great Park—Mercie and Caretaker were his true parents.

Simon Sinek's bestselling book, *Start with Why*,[32] advocates that the Why of a person or project is the starting point for success. The Why keeps the purpose and the goal in focus. Sinek recognizes the problems of mission and vision drift that so easily pull us away from our initial purpose and goal. When we lose the Why, we lose the energy that set everything in motion. "Start with Why" is, indeed, a powerful principle for effectiveness and success.

But in fact, Why flows from Who. We must start with Who. Identity is the essence of our perception of reality, the framework for motivation (our Why), the foundation for our purpose, and the basis for our measures of both meaning and success.

People of faith also include the ultimate Who of the universe and beyond: God. That leads us to frame our identity in the context of both who we are and whose we are. Even as citizens identify themselves as belonging to a particular nation, and as employees identify themselves as belonging to or being part of a corporation, so faith-based people identify themselves as part of the body of Christ and participants in God's coming kingdom.

This leads to the most basic question: Who tells you who you are?

12
Who Tells You Who You Are?

In his book *American Dream: Lost & Found*, American writer, historian, actor, and broadcaster Louis "Studs" Terkel wrote about a time he was riding in a taxi in St. Louis.

> During the Christmas bombings of North Vietnam, the St. Louis cabbie, weaving his way through traffic, was offering six o'clock commentary.
>
> "We gotta do it. We have no choice."
>
> "Why?"
>
> "We can't be a pitiful, helpless giant. We gotta show 'em we're number one."
>
> "Are you number one?"
>
> A pause. "I'm number nothin'." He recounts a litany of personal troubles, grievances, and disasters. His wife left him; his daughter is a roundheel; his boy is hooked on heroin; he loathes his job. For that matter, he's not so crazy about himself. Wearied by this turn of conversation, he addresses the rear-view mirror: "Did you hear Bob Hope last night? He said…"
>
> Forfeiting their own life experience, their native intelligence, their personal pride, they allow more celebrated surrogates, whose imaginations may be no larger than theirs, to think for them, to speak for them, to be for them in the name of the greater good.[33]

This taxi driver's blunt self-assessment takes our breath away. "I'm number nothin'." Like the taxi driver, we usually use external reference points both to define us and to validate us. He defined himself in terms of family disappointments and failures. We also define ourselves by other factors such as race, gender, belief system, economic status, locale, and family lineage.

We validate ourselves by achievements, institutions of higher learning, corporations, affiliations, bank account balances, stock portfolios, number of followers, balance sheets, friend requests, sales figures, calendar appointments, and invitations. The list goes on and on.

What's on your self-validation list?

Our reference points too often supersede God's value system.

I was part of a what we called a "renewal team" that came together from several churches to present a weekend of spiritual inspiration and renewal to a congregation in northeastern Ohio. Since many of us had never met, we went around the circle to introduce ourselves.

The first person, a well-known pastor, had come to preach. The second person, a well-known musician, would provide an opening concert and lead worship. The next person was a surgeon known for her exceptional skill and deep faith. She would share her faith journey.

The next person spoke quietly: "My name is Joe. I'm 'justa' contractor and layman in my church."

As he spoke, I felt something inside me snap. Before I knew it, I heard myself say, "Joe, there's no such person as a 'justa!'" Joe looked puzzled, then he smiled. And the group started to laugh.

In God's eyes, there's no such person as "justa" laywoman, "justa" layman," "justa" pastor, "justa" youth worker, or "justa" retired person. There are no justas! Every person has been created by God with a unique call.

That applies to *you*, too. God created you to do what only you can do!

God tells us who we are. "See what kind of love the Father has given to us, that we should be called children of God; and *so we are*. The reason why the world does not know us is that it did not know him. Beloved, *we are God's children now* (1 John 3:1-2, ESV emphasis added).

But deep down, many of us have not internalized this truth. We fail to grasp our true value and identity in Christ because we listen to the seductive voices of the world.

13

The World Says,
"You Are What You DO"

The world of everyday life has an enormous impact on how we identify ourselves. Four voices speak loudly ... and deceptively.

First, the world says, "You Are What You DO." This is the voice of performance-based identity.

Of course, there is a place for performance and accomplishment. God created us to exercise responsible governance over creation (Genesis 1:26-30). We work, we serve, and we do things to make life better for ourselves and others. The New Testament affirms the value of our contribution:

> For we are God's handiwork, created in Christ Jesus to do good works, which God prepared in advance for us to do" (Ephesians 2:10, NIV).

Or, as we read in another translation:

> "For we are God's masterpiece. He has created us anew in Christ Jesus, so we can do the good things he planned for us long ago" (NLT).

Scripture also rebukes those who can work but who refuse to do so:

> For you yourselves know how you ought to follow our example. We were not idle when we were with you, nor did we eat anyone's food without paying for it. On the contrary, we worked night and day, laboring and toiling so that we would not be a burden to any of you. We did this, not because we do not have the right to such help, but in order to offer ourselves as a model for you to imitate. For even when we were with you, we gave you this rule: "The one who is unwilling to work shall not eat" (2 Thessalonians 3:7-10, NIV).

The problem arises when our work becomes the primary basis for our self-worth. We suffer grave consequences when we equate our identity with our productivity.

We miscalculate our worth based on productivity and "usefulness."

The productivity factor says that our worth equals our work, that our value depends on our usefulness, and that we derive our significance from our performance.

Self + Productivity = Identity.

This seems to be the intrinsic motivation behind our work ethic, though it need not be so. Joyful stewardship is a *far* more effective stimulus than anxious performance.

The logic of productivity is heartless. It casts a cold, dark shadow over too many lives. What of those physically or mentally challenged from birth or illness? What about children and older people unable to contribute "measurable" productivity to society? What happens when the business doesn't succeed, or we lose our job? When we stop and evaluate these situations, no one with a heart would say those affected have no value. Yet we often fail to see the logic of productivity that oppresses our own lives. If we can see the irrationality of applying the utility factor to others, why can't we extend the same grace toward ourselves?

I know what it means to be haunted by the dark principality of productivity. I get restless when I sit still for too long. I feel like I need to be doing *something* worthwhile, otherwise I am just wasting oxygen. Sad!

Tim Hansel's book title says it so well: *When I Relax, I Feel Guilty.* Hansel sounds a warning to performance-driven individuals. He speaks with soul-rattling insight, especially as he uncovers the distorted theological rationale that drives so many of Jesus' followers. He writes,

> In our worthy attempt to avoid idleness and questionable pleasures, we begin to feel that everything must be useful. Thus, our false guilt compels us to read for profit, attend parties for contacts, exercise so we can work better, and rest in order to be more efficient. We regress to a kind of neopuritanism that says, "You have not been born into the world for pleasure." A curious and familiar psychological need to justify everything emerges, leaving no room for discovery and pure enjoyment.[34]

A productivity-based identity generates multiple problems of pride, anxiety, devaluing others, and even despair.

1.   PRIDE PLAGUES A PRODUCTIVITY-BASED IDENTITY.

Pride is the most obvious problem for those who feel confident in their accomplishments. We may feel an appropriate sense of satisfaction in the effort we expend and the results we may be privileged to witness. But the wise disciple knows the truth that Paul proclaimed about his own ministry:

> I planted the seed, Apollos watered it, but God has been making it grow. So, neither the one who plants nor the one who waters is anything, but only God, who makes things grow. The one who plants and the one who waters have one purpose, and they will each be rewarded according to their own labor. For we are co-workers in God's service; you are God's field, God's building (1 Corinthians 3:6-9, NIV).

Paul was quick to rebuke boasting, especially in the context of affirming our partnership with the Lord:

> For it is by grace you have been saved, through faith—and this is not from yourselves, it is the gift of God— not by works, so that no one can boast. For we are God's handiwork, created in Christ Jesus to do good works, which God prepared in advance for us to do (Ephesians 2:8-10, NIV).

Pride has no place in a disciple's heart and mind. "What do you have that you did not receive? And if you did receive it, why do you boast as though you did not?" (1 Corinthians 4:7, NIV)

When someone boasts about pulling themselves up by their own bootstraps, I often ask, "Where did you get the boots?" We could even be more direct and inquire where they received the hands, feet, and opportunity to wear boots!

2.   ANXIETY HAUNTS A PRODUCTIVITY-BASED IDENTITY.

Feeling the need to continually prove our worth is like running on a never-ending treadmill. When have we done enough? Who needs to know and approve? What's next? Am I meeting all the expectations?

In a context of continual productivity, Jesus' invitation in Matthew 11:28-30 makes no sense:

> Come to me, all you who are weary and burdened, and I will give you rest. Take my yoke upon you and learn from me, for I am gentle and humble in heart, and you will find rest for your souls. For my yoke is easy and my burden is light. (NIV)

Eugene Peterson's unique phrasing of this passage deeply moves many of us:

Are you tired? Worn out? Burned out on religion? Come to me. Get away with me and you'll recover your life. I'll show you how to take a real rest. Walk with me and work with me—watch how I do it. Learn the unforced rhythms of grace. I won't lay anything heavy or ill-fitting on you. Keep company with me and you'll learn to live freely and lightly. (*The Message*)

By God's grace in Jesus Christ, we do not calculate our worth based on our ability to produce a significant ROI (Return on Investment). As we will see in Part Three, we *do* play a role in God's continuing mission in this world—but that is the *motivation* for our work, not the *basis* for our worth. That's why Paul gives us the calm-inducing, breath-catching promise of Philippians 4:6-7:

Don't worry about anything; instead, pray about everything. Tell God what you need and thank him for all he has done. Then you will experience God's peace, which exceeds anything we can understand. His peace will guard your hearts and minds as you live in Christ Jesus (NLT).

Thankfulness puts everything into perspective. Even when we don't fully understand the nature of our situation, we are thankful for God's presence, power, and provision in our situation.

3.   DEVALUING OTHERS ACCOMPANIES A PRODUCTIVITY-BASED IDENTITY.

When we feel tempted to measure worth in terms of accomplishments, awards, and attention, we tend to turn people into projects. We love people for what they do for us, rather than for who they are.

This transactional view of relationships robs all involved of safety and vulnerability. We feel forced to live behind a façade of success, a mask of invincibility—and we expect the same of others.

4.   DISCOURAGEMENT AND DESPAIR FOLLOWS A PRODUCTIVITY-BASED IDENTITY.

Our performance is uneven and can easily be disrupted. No one is perfect. Everyone makes mistakes. And, sometimes, those mistakes are huge. What happens to your identity when you cannot lean on your impressive record of accomplishments?

How to Release a Productivity-based Identity

The surest way to release a productivity-based identity is to acknowledge your imperfection and focus on Jesus' grace.

François Fénelon, a seventeenth century Archbishop of Cambrai, France, served in the court of Louis XIV, also known as Louis the Great or the Sun King (1643-1715 AD). Fénelon often provided spiritual direction to noblemen and ladies in the king's court. His counsel on imperfection and failure reveals wisdom that liberates us from performance anxiety:

> The way I see the problem is this: I think you really do want God to be glorified in your life, but you think this is going to be accomplished by becoming more and more perfect. And in doing this you still are thinking of your own personal worth.
>
> So, if you would truly desire profit from the discovery of your imperfections, I would suggest two things. First of all, never try to justify yourself before God. And second, do not condemn yourself. Instead, why not quietly lay your imperfections before God?
>
> Do not be overly concerned about your defects. Instead concentrate on having an unceasing love for Jesus, and you shall be much forgiven because you have loved much (Lk 7:47).
>
> When we look at our defects in peace through the spirit of Jesus, they vanish before the majesty of His love. But when we concentrate on our defects, forgetting that Jesus loves us, we become restless, the presence of God is interrupted, and the flow of God's love is hindered. The humiliation we feel about our own defects can often be a greater fault than the original defect itself if it keeps you from moving into the realization of God's love.[35]

Remember how God the Father affirmed Jesus' identity at His Son's baptism:

> …the Holy Spirit descended on him in bodily form, like a dove; and a voice came from heaven, "You are my beloved Son; with you I am well pleased" (Luke 3:22, NIV).

Before any formal ministry achievement, before any great sermon or teaching, before any miracles were accomplished, God affirmed Jesus' identity and value. Jesus' identity was "fixed" and secure from beginning.

Likewise, our identity is based on our God-imputed intrinsic value. It is not conditional, based on productivity and performance.

Remember Paul's words:

> For all who are led by the Spirit of God are children of God. So, you have not received a spirit that makes you fearful slaves. Instead, you received God's Spirit when he adopted you as his own children. Now we call him, "Abba, Father." For his Spirit joins with our spirit to affirm that we are God's children. And since we are his children, we are his heirs. In fact, together with Christ we are heirs of God's glory. But if we are to share his glory, we must also share his suffering. (Romans 8:14-17, NLT).

In Christ, we have received grace that establishes our intrinsic value. We can say, "I am loved for who I am in Christ, not on the basis of what I do."

Who You Are Does Not Depend on What You Do

In his book *Leadership Prayers*, Dr. Richard Kriegbaum talks about his experience as president of a Christian university in California's central valley. One day a mother and daughter excoriated him because they felt misled about the university's housing and financial aid. He wrote,

> My empathy for them was sincere, my inner spirit at peace. Why? Because I was able to separate my basic identity from my leadership role… Whenever I base my identity or worth as a person on my role as a leader, I betray myself and miss God's best for me. I am not inherently the leader. I am God's child whom he dearly loves whether people are pleased or angry with my decisions, whether I succeed or fail.[36]

In the prayer he composed to accompany this reflection, Kriegbaum prays,

> Please help me keep it straight. Leadership is extremely important, and I want intensely to do it right, but sometimes I forget where the role ends and I start. So, I want you to remind me, however and whenever you have to… *It's not really me, God. It's just what I do.*"[37]

What we do (or fail to do) does not ultimately define us. Our being precedes our doing. Our doing flows from our being. And God's grace comes to us at the starting line.

14
The World Says, "You Are What You OWN"

The world also tells us, "You are what you own." This second declaration is the voice of possessions-based identity.

In a consumer society, possessions communicate status. What you have signals your worth and importance.

Self + Impressive Stuff = Identity.

Of course, having nice things isn't wrong. Money and possessions aren't inherently evil. Scripture affirms the goodness of creation, which includes personal property. God called creation good (see Genesis 1:4, 10, 12) and provided generously for all creatures, especially human beings. We are free to enjoy the goodness given to us by our good God.

Many often misunderstand spirituality as asceticism, or abstinence from worldly pleasures. While it's true that spirituality can include ascetic practices such as fasting, we usually practice these occasionally; they are not a permanent condition of living.[38] The following passage affirms the blessing of what we could call "ordinary life."

> Now the Spirit expressly says that in later times some will depart from the faith by devoting themselves to deceitful spirits and teachings of demons, through the insincerity of liars whose consciences are seared, who forbid marriage and require abstinence from foods that God created to be received with thanksgiving by those who believe and know the truth. *For everything created by God is good, and nothing is to be rejected if it is received with thanksgiving, for it is made holy by the word of God and prayer* (1 Timothy 4:4-5, ESV emphasis added).

Problems arise when the things of this world become the basis for how we feel about and value ourselves.

1. A POSSESSIONS-BASED IDENTITY OFTEN RESULTS IN DISSATISFACTION, NOT CONTENTMENT.

The first consequence of a possessions-based identity is the

"Ecclesiastes syndrome" of discontent and disillusionment. It's worth quoting extensively here from Solomon's reflections to show the scope of his material attainments … and the depth of his disillusionment.

> I said to myself, "Come on, let's try pleasure. Let's look for the 'good things' in life." But I found that this, too, was meaningless. So, I said, "Laughter is silly. What good does it do to seek pleasure?" After much thought, I decided to cheer myself with wine. And while still seeking wisdom, I clutched at foolishness. In this way, I tried to experience the only happiness most people find during their brief life in this world.

> I also tried to find meaning by building huge homes for myself and by planting beautiful vineyards. I made gardens and parks, filling them with all kinds of fruit trees. I built reservoirs to collect the water to irrigate my many flourishing groves. I bought slaves, both men and women, and others were born into my household. I also owned large herds and flocks, more than any of the kings who had lived in Jerusalem before me. I collected great sums of silver and gold, the treasure of many kings and provinces. I hired wonderful singers, both men and women, and had many beautiful concubines. I had everything a man could desire!

> So I became greater than all who had lived in Jerusalem before me, and my wisdom never failed me. Anything I wanted, I would take. I denied myself no pleasure. I even found great pleasure in hard work, a reward for all my labors. But as I looked at everything I had worked so hard to accomplish, it was all so meaningless—like chasing the wind. There was nothing really worthwhile anywhere (Ecclesiastes 2:1-12, NLT).

Naturally, at times we'd all say, "I'd like to have the opportunity Solomon had (with some notable exceptions like slaves and multiple wives and concubines!!) —and then see if I'd be so discouraged!" But we've all had the experience of getting something new or special, only to have the excitement quickly fade. What we once treasured, we now take for granted. The more we get, the more we want. It's like drinking salt water: instead of quenching our thirst, we just crave more.

2.   A POSSESSIONS-BASED IDENTITY FOSTERS MATERIALISM, WHICH
     UNDERMINES GENEROSITY AND STEWARDSHIP.

The Bible clearly tells us that God blesses us so that we may bless others. The Lord told Abram (later Abraham) in Genesis 12:1-3(NIV):

> The LORD had said to Abram, "Go from your country, your people and your father's household to the land I will show you.

> "I will make you into a great nation,

> and I will bless you;
> I will make your name great,

> and you will be a blessing.
> I will bless those who bless you,
> and whoever curses you I will curse;
> and all peoples on earth
> will be blessed through you."

God has woven a holy cycle of blessing into the very fiber of life. He blesses us so we will bless others, who will bless others, who will… you get the idea. *We* are the primary means God uses to communicate and channel His resources to others. As Paul wrote in 2 Corinthians 9:11 (NIV), "You will be enriched in every way so that you can be generous on every occasion, and through us your generosity will result in thanksgiving to God."

Proverbs 11:24-25 states,

> "One person gives freely, yet gains even more; another withholds unduly, but comes to poverty. A generous person will prosper; whoever refreshes others will be refreshed"(NIV).

Puritan John Bunyan expressed the same principle this way:

> There was a man, the world did think him mad,
> The more he gave away the more he had.

One day a beggar by the roadside asked for alms from Alexander the Great as he passed by. The man, of course, had no claim upon the ruler, yet the emperor threw several gold coins to him. A courtier, astonished at his generosity, asked Alexander, "Sir, copper coins would have adequately met a beggar's need. Why give him gold?"

Alexander responded, "Copper coins would suit the beggar's need, but gold coins suit Alexander's giving."

While I cannot cite specific sources, I have read many studies (almost annually) that claim the wealthy give less proportionately than those who have less. But we all need to give. Giving awakens our gratitude. We become more alert and sensitive to human beings and circumstances around us. We learn to hold our resources more loosely, more lightly, and more freely.

3.   A POSSESSIONS-BASED IDENTITY COMPROMISES OUR WITNESS TO GOD'S KINGDOM VALUES.

Does our use of our money demonstrate our allegiance to God's Kingdom? Is it obvious that we serve God and not mammon?

Our use of money significantly expresses our testimony. It should be clear to everyone that we lead a life of generosity. C. S. Lewis writes:

> Charity is an essential part of Christian morality… I do not believe one can settle how much we ought to give. I am afraid the only safe rule is to give more than we can spare. In other words, if our expenditure on comforts, luxuries, amusements, etc., is up to the standard common among those with the same income as our own, we are probably giving away too little. If our charities do not at all pinch or hamper us, I should say they are too small. There ought to be things we should like to do and cannot do because our charitable expenditure excludes them.[39]

Our Identity in Christ Enables Us to Thrive with Contentment

Our humble trust in our value as God's child generates a spirit of contentment. We enjoy the possessions of this world without being possessed by them.

The danger from wildfires in southern California consistently reminds me that physical things are transitory. They can literally be here today and burned to ashes tomorrow. You can't put much in an emergency evacuation "Go Bag!" The general advice is to take only the irreplaceable items, often grouped under the headings People, Pets, Papers (like passports, insurance policies), Prescriptions, and Photos (irreplaceable mementos).

Contentment and celebration also displace the comparison and competition that devour peace of mind and undermine relationships. "There is great gain in godliness combined with contentment" (1 Timothy 6:6, NRSVue). Paul also describes the liberating power of a contentment mindset:

> Not that I am speaking of being in need, for I have learned
> in whatever situation I am to be content. I know how to be
> brought low, and I know how to abound. In any and every
> circumstance, I have learned the secret of facing plenty and
> hunger, abundance and need. I can do all things through him
> who strengthens me (Philippians 4:11-13, ESV).

We trust in God's provision and cultivate contentment because we
know that where God guides, God provides.

15
The World Says, "You Are Who You KNOW"

The world continually declares to us, "You are who you KNOW." This is the voice of popularity-based identity.

We often rely on our personality and social connections for our identity and sense of self-worth. This includes our desire to make a good impression on people, to be included, to belong, to be valued by others.

Self + People's Opinions and Support = Identity.

Of course, networks and connections are wonderful. Relationships matter. We are to love our neighbor as ourselves and to care for one another. But several problems arise when we base our worth on our relationships and popularity, on who invites us to what events, or on whose name we can "name-drop" in conversations.

1. POPULARITY-BASED IDENTITY TRIES TO LINK OUR WORTH TO "IMPORTANT" PEOPLE.

I use a personal pun to describe this tendency, calling it "gilt by association."[40] You're likely familiar with the phrase "guilt by association," when the people associated with a guilty person are judged guilty because of their association—even if their "guilt" is unfounded. "Gilt" by association is just the reverse. Gilt by association refers to the effort of trying to shine in the glow of another person's importance.

Gilt is gold leaf or gold paint applied in a thin layer to some surface. It is a decorative feature, meant to give the impression of value and even "solid gold." It's all about impressing others. I fall into this when I "name drop" about people I know or who attend my church, or "place-drop" about places I've been in my travels. You get the idea. You can recognize it quickly in others but seldom see it in yourself.

2. POPULARITY-BASED IDENTITY VIEWS PEOPLE AS OBJECTS AND AS

A MEANS TO OUR END

We are to value people for themselves, not for what we can get from them. And we are to value ourselves based on God's declaration of our worth. When we objectify others, we stop seeing them as unique image-bearers of God and instead see them as a means to our own satisfaction.

We also become the victims of this attitude in others. You can tell this dynamic is at work when you have a "close friendship" for a season that suddenly ends. Why does it end? Often it is because your "friend" has gotten what they wanted from you and moved on.

As leaders, we're all aware of those who engage with us only because of some agenda. They want to be close to us for their own advancement. They want to glean specific information from us for their own prestige. "I was talking with the CEO the other day, and she said she was really concerned about…"

Agenda-based relationships will always exist on our fallen planet. Wisdom requires us to recognize them and not allow ourselves to reduce others to pawns in our game. We value individuals for who they are and for the necessary role they play in our lives.

3.   POPULARITY-BASED IDENTITY DRIVES US TO CHASE WORLDLY RECOGNITION

Most of us fall far short of achieving value and recognition in the eyes of the world. Listen to Paul's blunt assessment of some Corinthian followers of Jesus:

> For consider your calling, brothers: not many of you were wise according to worldly standards, not many were powerful, not many were of noble birth…. And because of him you are in Christ Jesus, who became to us wisdom from God, righteousness and sanctification and redemption, so that, as it is written, "Let the one who boasts, boast in the Lord" (1 Corinthians 1:26-31, ESV).

Popularity is fleeting. In our poll-saturated culture, celebrities and politicians rise and fall at dramatic rates. Likewise, a person who links their worth to others' opinions and perceptions will have a constantly shifting sense of value. We need a reference point beyond fickle humanity. Our reference point is our identity as God's children:

"The Spirit himself bears witness with our spirit that we are children of God, and if children, then heirs—heirs of God and fellow heirs with Christ" (Romans 8:16-17 ESV).

No one we know can add to that; no one we don't know can detract from that.

16
The World Says,
"You Are Your POSITION"

When did you last hear the world tell you, "You are your TITLE"? This is the voice of position-based identity, which bases your worth on your status. It insists, "You are your rank, your title, your office."

Self + Position = Identity.

The issue of position has many layers. *Of course*, position matters. We value and respect appropriate rank and status. Higher positions enable us to accomplish valuable goals and to exert influence in ways that further our kingdom values. We can be stewards who can utilize human, intellectual, and capital resources to make an impact.

The problem arises when we equate our position with our value. This voice tempts us with the most obvious self-serving benefits of power and control. And, as with all the other "identity falsehoods" the world tells us, this one comes with several problems.

1. POSITION-BASED IDENTITY MISTAKES OUR POSITION FOR OUR PERSON

We must separate what we do from who we are. It was always more helpful for me to say, "I am a child of God who preaches," than to say, "I am a preacher." Why? Because what I do is just one aspect of who I am. We can apply this same principle to all fields of endeavor:

"I am a child of God who serves the Lord as a sales team leader."

"I am a child of God who serves the Lord as a regional manager."

"I am a child of God who serves the Lord as a teacher."

"I am a child of God who serves the Lord as the president of a corporation."

Notice that we make the distinction between who we are and what we do.

This is even more significant if we leave a prominent position through resignation or even by termination. At times in life, individuals must face the tough choice between the ever-increasing demands of work and the ever-increasing demands of family or personal life.

An illness, a family crisis, or a change in company priorities, values, or direction are among the factors that can generate a decision to step *down* (the direction is significant) from a high position. What happens to a person's identity when he or she says, "I used to be CFO, but I stepped out…"?

Termination can also trigger an identity crisis. In addition to managing feelings of shame, embarrassment, even self-condemnation, individuals often begin to realize, "I'm not sure who I am anymore without that title, that position, that status…"

2. POSITION-BASED IDENTITY SPARKS COMPETITION AND COMPARISON THAT STIMULATE EITHER OUR PRIDE OR OUR INSECURITY.

The direction we choose to look for measuring ourselves can lead either to pride or insecurity. Both undermine our relationships and can devour our peace of mind.

Competition and comparison usually manifest themselves in envy, covetousness, and jealousy. The meanings of envy and jealousy can easily be confused. Ben-Ze'ev writes:

> *Envy*: The emotional attitude of wishing to have what someone else has, which is important for the person's self-definition.

> *Jealousy*: The emotional attitude of wishing not to lose something (typically, a favorable human relationship), which is important for the person's self-definition to someone else.[41]

Zev continues by arguing that an individual's exclusive relationship is often a factor in jealousy. The object of jealousy cannot be generically replaced:

> Hence, jealousy is often concerned with exclusiveness. Envy, on the other hand, is concerned with inequality. Jealousy is concerned with rivalry while envy is concerned with inferiority. Romantic love, therefore, may produce jealousy. The jealous person is often interested in maintaining the present situation while the envious person often desires something new; envy is almost always considered a moral flaw while jealousy can be legitimate.[42]

A legitimate expression of jealousy is God's righteous jealousy for our exclusive devotion. "You shall not bow down to them or worship them; for I, the LORD your God, am a jealous God" (Exodus 20:5, NIV). God rightfully demands absolute allegiance and loyalty from those He has loved and redeemed.

Following His resurrection, Jesus bluntly addressed competition in His redemptive conversation with Peter, as recorded in John 21. Jesus asked Peter three times, "Do you love me?" He was giving Peter three opportunities to "un-speak" his earlier three denials (John 21:15-17). Then the Lord gave Peter a cryptic description of the "death by which he would glorify God." Here's Peter's response:

> Peter turned and saw that the disciple whom Jesus loved was following them. (This was the one who had leaned back against Jesus at the supper and had said, "Lord, who is going to betray you?") When Peter saw him, he asked, "Lord, what about him?"
>
> Jesus answered, *"If I want him to remain alive until I return, what is that to you? You must follow me"* (John 21:20-22, NIV, emphasis added).

To be candid, Jesus put Peter in his place. At the same time, Jesus gave us the best advice to break the spell of comparison and competition. When we feel the tug of envy or resentment at another's prosperity, recognition, or success, we need to remind ourselves bluntly, "What is that to me? I must follow Jesus."

Our Identity in Christ Enables Us to Thrive with Humility

Perhaps you've come across the poem "The Indispensable Man," by Saxon White Kessinger. (By the way, if you struggle with the title, it might be important to note that Kessinger was a woman). If you haven't read the poem, you are likely familiar with two couplets from it:

> Take a bucket and fill it with water,
> Put your hand in it up to the wrist,
> Pull it out and the hole that's remaining,
> Is a measure of how much you'll be missed.[43]

Dwight D. Eisenhower (Ike), the five-star general who served as the Supreme Allied Commander in World War II and who later became U.S. President, carried a copy of this poem in his pocket from the time it was published. "In fact," bloggers Brett & Kate McKay write, "when Ike returned to Normandy for the 20th anniversary of D-Day and was asked to give a speech at a dinner commemorating the invasion, rather than use the occasion to wax poetic about his role in executing one of the most monumental military operations in history, this man of singular eminence instead used the opportunity to read 'The Indispensable Man'."[44]

As sobering as it is to face the stark reality that none of us is indispensable, it's also a huge relief. Only God is indispensable! The sooner we realize that, the more freedom and joy we'll find.

Humility is realizing, first, that we are not God. Second, it's being content with our position in life. I heard the following story in a seminary class on world missions from my professor, J. Christy Wilson:

> Two military officers were talking at an official dinner at which William Carey, the famous British missionary, was present. One of the officers said to the other, "Wasn't Carey just a shoemaker before he became a missionary?"
>
> Carey overheard their conversation. He interrupted and said, "Excuse me, sir, but I was just a cobbler. I only mended shoes; I didn't make them."

That's humility: freedom from the need to make an impression on others because Christ has made His impression on you.

True humility is more of an attitude toward others than an attitude toward ourselves.

Think of the person who looks up from a hospital bed into the eyes of the surgeon who saved the person's life. The patient in bed is humbled. That humility is not self-depreciation, nor self-degradation, nor self-anything. It's the humility expressed in overwhelming gratitude to the one who saved the person's life. She brags with joy about the surgeon's power that brought her through the dangers. Her face beams and eyes glisten with the inarticulate wonder of being cared for by another.

When I humble myself, I do not become a doormat for someone else to abuse; rather, I become a doorway for others to enter the place of affirmation and value. Humility does not mean I think less of myself, but that I think more of you.

Our Identity in Christ Enables us to Thrive Apart from Our Position

This concept goes to the very heart of who we are and how we see ourselves. Let me state the premise again: *Our identity in Christ enables us to thrive apart from our position in any organization.* It's too easy to read these words without allowing them to sink in. Our spiritual well-being does not depend on our vocational status.

Jesus' disciples wrestled with the siren call of such seductive, worldly voices. James and John, the sons of Zebedee, bluntly voiced their ambition to Jesus: "Appoint us to sit, one at your right hand and one at your left, in your glory" (Mark 10:37, ESV). When Jesus politely declined their request, word got out to the other disciples.

> And when the ten heard it, they began to be indignant at James and John. And Jesus called them to Him and said to them, "You know that those who are considered rulers of the Gentiles lord it over them, and their great ones exercise authority over them. But it shall not be so among you. But whoever would be great among you must be your servant, and whoever would be first among you must be slave of all. *For even the Son of Man came not to be served but to serve, and to give his life as a ransom for many*" (Mark 10:41-45, ESV, emphasis added).

Jesus used his position to further God's mission. God's mission, not Jesus' position, was primary.

In Acts 1:6-8, following Jesus' resurrection but before His ascension, the disciples still felt preoccupied with a worldly view of their work. They still anticipated receiving a reward as part of an earthly, political kingdom.

> So, when they had come together, they asked him, "Lord, is this the time when you will restore the kingdom to Israel?" He replied, "It is not for you to know the times or periods that the Father has set by his own authority. But you will receive power when the Holy Spirit has come upon you, and you will be my witnesses in Jerusalem, in all Judea and Samaria, and to the ends of the earth" (NRSVue).

Jesus turned their focus from worldly success to spiritual witness. They were to share what God had done, not give their energies to their own advancement.

Identity is who we are in Christ apart from everything else. So, what are the specific elements of our identity? That's our next question.

17
Identity Is Received, Not Achieved

How does Jesus define us? Let's start with Jesus' teaching on identity from His Sermon on the Mount. That sermon summarizes Jesus' teaching on living for the kingdom of God: or as Matthew says, "the kingdom of heaven."

Jesus creates a kingdom community based on different measures of what matters. Jesus' followers are to be a different people.

Christ begins with the "great reversals" of the Beatitudes, where we discover we are blessed when we least expect it. Then, in Matthew 5:13-16—immediately following the Beatitudes—Jesus calls us to show others the difference that living in and for God's kingdom makes.

> *You are the salt of the earth*. But if the salt loses its saltiness, how can it be made salty again? It is no longer good for anything, except to be thrown out and trampled underfoot.

> *"You are the light of the world*. A town built on a hill cannot be hidden. Neither do people light a lamp and put it under a bowl. Instead, they put it on its stand, and it gives light to everyone in the house. In the same way, let your light shine before others, that they may see your good deeds and glorify your Father in heaven (Matthew 5:13-16, NIV, emphasis added).

Notice what Jesus *doesn't* say. He does not say, "If you try hard enough, maybe you'll be like salt and light." He does not say, "I hope you guys will at least *try* to make a difference in this world, like salt and light do." The Master does not say, "Wouldn't it be great if a few of my followers really took this stuff seriously and lived like salt and light in this world?"

No. Jesus declares, "You are the salt of the earth" and "You are the light of the world."

These are declarative statements that assert truth. They are not aspirational statements of some hoped-for reality. They state present circumstances, not future possibilities. Jesus announces our identity.

This is the glory and the mystery of the Christian life! Through faith in Jesus Christ, we receive a new self, a new identity, which depends not on what we can achieve but on what we are willing to receive. "I am not the esteem, I can collect through competition, but the love I have freely received from God," Henri Nouwen said.[45]

Before we explore the implications of being salt and light, let's linger for a moment on the implications of Jesus' declaration. First, we must listen first, only, and always to God's voice.

God Tells You *Who* You Are

We listen not to the seductive voices of the world but to the authoritative, definitive voice of the God who created us in His own image.

One way to make Scripture come alive in a personal way is to paraphrase it in the first person, as if God were speaking personally to you and about you. A first-person paraphrase of Genesis 1:26-28 (in which I will include my wife, Sarah, for obvious reasons) could read like this:

> Then God said, "Let us make Doug and Sarah in our image, to be like us. They will reign over the fish in the sea, the birds in the sky, the livestock, all the wild animals on the earth, and the small animals that scurry along the ground."
>
> So God created Doug and Sarah in his own image.
>
> In the image of God he created them;
>
> male and female he created them.

Let's continue this exercise with another passage:

> Doug, God saved you by his grace when you believed. And you can't take credit for this; it is a gift from God. Salvation is not a reward for the good things you have done, Doug, so you cannot boast about it. For, Doug, you are God's masterpiece. He has created you anew in Christ Jesus, so you can do the good things He planned for you long ago" (Ephesians 2:8-10, paraphrased).

According to those verses, my identity is defined by grace, for which I am grateful. It is not based on any accomplishments for which I might try to boast. It's about what God has done for me, not what I've done for God.

A second feature of my identity is that I am "God's masterpiece." The Greek word *poema* is the same word from which we derive the

English word "poem." A poem is characterized by highly crafted writing. Every word is carefully chosen to provide compressed meaning and impact.

One example of poetic craftsmanship that has always touched me is *God's Grandeur*, by Gerard Manley Hopkins (1844 –1889).[46] Hopkins was a Jesuit priest whose poems were not published until after his death. The opening lines of this poem convey, as poet Stanley Kunitz said, "lyric passion, so fierce, yet eloquent, wounded, yet radiant."[47]

> The world is charged with the grandeur of God.
> It will flame out, like shining from shook foil;
> It gathers to a greatness, like the ooze of oil
> Crushed.

I encourage you to look up the poem and read the whole piece for yourself. The point is that God has handcrafted us with the care, intention, and creativity of a master poet. We are not assembly line products mass produced for generic use! We are sculptured, tailored, shaped for a unique purpose by God's expertise and artistry.

This theme of being a handcrafted treasure is echoed in Psalm 139:13-16 (ESV):

> For you formed my inward parts;
> you knitted me together in my mother's womb.
> I praise you, for I am fearfully and wonderfully made.
> Wonderful are your works;
> my soul knows it very well.
> My frame was not hidden from you,
> when I was being made in secret,
> intricately woven in the depths of the earth.
> Your eyes saw my unformed substance;
> in your book were written, every one of them,
> the days that were formed for me,
> when as yet there was none of them.

The psalmist does not assert that God has written a detailed script designed to control the events of our lives. He uses the image of a book to express his confidence and comfort in the fact of God's providential involvement and care in his life.

Scripture clearly teaches that you are not a mistake, an accident, or a product of blind chance. You are here "on purpose" for God's purpose and your joy.

Your identity, therefore, is directed toward the purpose and the works that God planned long ago for you to do. Grace precedes performance; it does not eliminate it.

Our identity is interwoven with our destiny to govern creation (to be explored more fully in Part Two).

God Tells You *Whose* You Are

Where does your ultimate allegiance lie? Who or what claims your loyalty? We all have lesser allegiances to our schools, communities, state, nation, and family, from which we derive a sense of identity and belonging. But is there something bigger?

Jesus' followers know they belong to God's Kingdom. Paul reminds us, in stark terms:

> "Or do you not know that your body is a temple of the Holy Spirit within you, whom you have from God? You are not your own, for you were bought with a price. So glorify God in your body" (1 Corinthians 6:19-20, ESV).

Knowing whose we are anchors our identity outside ourselves. We're part of a much bigger entity. Even as an alum of a great university draws on the prestige of that institution, so we draw on our citizenship in God's kingdom.

As much as we want to assert our independence, we cannot sustain ourselves without countless sources of support. Ultimately, God determines our days.

> Come now, you who say, "Today or tomorrow we will go into such and such a town and spend a year there and trade and make a profit"—yet you do not know what tomorrow will bring. What is your life? For you are a mist that appears for a little time and then vanishes. Instead, you ought to say, "If the Lord wills, we will live and do this or that." As it is, you boast in your arrogance. All such boasting is evil (James 4:13-16, ESV).

Consider three important implications of belonging to God.

1. KNOWING WE BELONG TO GOD SETS THE DIRECTION FOR OUR LIVES.

We surrender to God's direction for our lives. This does not mean we no longer take the initiative. Nor does it mean we have no ambition.

We eagerly pursue the greatest achievements and step out in faith to pursue the highest goals empowered by God's Spirit.

"There is no magic in small plans. When I consider my ministry, I think of the world. Anything less than that would not be worthy of Christ, nor of his will for my life."[48] God did not create us for small lives. God created us to live life to the max. That's in part what Jesus means by coming to give us abundant life (John 10:10).

2.   KNOWING WE BELONG TO GOD DEFINES OUR LIMITS.

At the end of the day, we are stewards and managers, not creators and owners. This is important news for those who struggle with an overactive sense of responsibility!

Pastor Keith Brown, who pastored First Presbyterian Church in Bethlehem, Pennsylvania, confessed, "I used to view God as a perfectionist who was never quite satisfied with my achievements. It took me quite a while to learn that God really isn't happy when we're working ourselves to death."

George McCausland, a Methodist pastor in Pittsburgh, helped Brown come to this understanding. "The greatest moment in my life," he told Brown, "was when I resigned as manager of the universe."[49]

Our view of God strongly influences our view of ourselves. If God is a perfectionist, then we must strive for perfection to be acceptable.[50] But, in fact, God knows we are made of dust (Psalm 103:14). Paul calls us jars of clay (2 Corinthians 4:7). We are saved and sustained on our journey by faith alone. The root of faith will, by the power of the Holy Spirit, produce the fruit of the Spirit. That fruit expresses, but is not condition for, our acceptance in Christ.

3.   KNOWING WE BELONG TO GOD RELIEVES OUR BURDENS.

Because we belong to God, we can rely on God's care and provision. Ultimately, our well-being lies in God's hands. Countless promises in Scripture assure us of God's sovereign love and support. "Seek the Kingdom of God above all else, and live righteously, and he will give you everything you need" (Matthew 6:33, NLT). Like a loving parent, God provides for His family. Like a wise general, God cares for His soldiers. Like a good employer, God provides for those who work for Him.

Were we to claim sole independence, we would quickly find ourselves overwhelmed by our responsibilities and at the end of our resources. When we realize we belong to God, we are energized for

His service and secure in His love.

While we know our work is important, we also know that we depend on the Lord. Psalm 127:1-2(NLT), attributed to Solomon, communicates God's essential role in our work:

> Unless the Lord builds a house,
> the work of the builders is wasted.
> Unless the Lord protects a city,
> guarding it with sentries will do no good.
> It is useless for you to work so hard
> from early morning until late at night,
> anxiously working for food to eat;
> for God gives rest to his loved ones.

Notice the conclusion the psalmist draws from the necessity of God's involvement: non- anxious rest! God's essential involvement does not lead us to resignation but to humble dependence.

Knowing we belong to God results in great relief. Although we have a part to play, it's a limited part. We gratefully acknowledge that God bears the ultimate responsibility. It's *not* all up to us!

18
Jesus Identifies Us First as Children of God

Jesus calls us the salt of the earth. He equips us to bring vitality in places of worldly blandness and preservation in places of decay, so that the world "may see your good deeds and glorify your Father in heaven."

The foundation for our identity is our adoption into God's family as sons and daughters. Being salt links us directly to "our Father in Heaven." Jesus makes this same assertion as He begins the Lord's Prayer, "*Our* Father…" Jesus sweeps us into His status as God's child. Admittedly, we can never participate in one unique quality of Jesus' Sonship. He alone is both fully God and fully human. But the amazing grace of God welcomes us, by faith, into God's family as His sons and daughters. In fact, the Bible calls us "royal heirs with Christ," a primary theme throughout the Gospels.

> But to all who did receive him, who believed in his name, he gave the right to become children of God, who were born, not of blood nor of the will of the flesh nor of the will of man, but of God (John 1:12-13, ESV).

Paul emphasizes the genuine intimacy of our relationship as children of God:

> For you did not receive the spirit of slavery to fall back into fear, but you have received the Spirit of adoption as sons, by whom we cry, "Abba! Father!" The Spirit himself bears witness with our spirit that we are children of God, and if children, then heirs—heirs of God and fellow heirs with Christ, provided we suffer with him in order that we may also be glorified with him (Romans 8:15-17, ESV).

We are no longer disinherited rebels cut off from our heavenly Father. We are beloved children! The implications of this salvation fact alone should stagger our imaginations and shape our every breath, every moment, every choice.

It's essential to understand that our doing flows from our being; our work flows out from our identity in Christ. That relationship is the priority and the source of who we are and all we do.

I was sitting in my study one morning, frustrated by the stacks of unread books that continued to grow as my time for reading contracted.

"Lord," I cried out, "how can I ever know enough to serve you properly? I'll never get caught up!"

Then a stillness came over me, as if the Lord said, "Doug, look at your library. Can you hold all those books? If you stacked them one on top of the other, could you carry them?"

"Of course not, Lord. I could hold only a few…"

"Then don't try to hold them. Hold only Me."

Refreshment and relief swept over my spirit. I realized that knowledge about God often becomes an obstacle to intimate fellowship with God. Abiding in Christ, being filled with the Holy Spirit, worshiping the Lord Almighty—these practices root our identity in ways nothing in this world can imitate or destroy.

From this place of saltiness, being seasoned by our identity in God's family, we become active, contributing family members. We carry on the "family business."

19

Jesus Identifies Us as Partners in God's Continuing Work

"Salt preserves, purifies, flavors, and kills."[51] Jesus could be called the salt of the earth, though He never used that designation for Himself. But He certainly spiced things up!

We can see how He preserved God's truth in His teaching, how He purified hearts by His call to repentance and showing of mercy and grace, how He flavored life with His joy, and how He defeated the powers of darkness in His life, death, resurrection, and ascension. We would do well to meditate deeply on these salty functions in Jesus' life—and in our own.

And here's the astounding strategy of Jesus: that we continue His work in His power! That takes my breath away! We are to be salt in this decaying world and light to overcome the darkness that holds lives captive.

Be Spice for Blandness

Salt both seasons and enhances food, much like we should do in all of life. But salt also stings when it touches a wound—again, like we will in our faithful witness.

When Jesus calls us "the salt of earth," He is entrusting a huge vision and responsibility to us. Jesus expects and equips us to make a significant difference in this world.

Jesus also warns us that we can "go flat," losing our saltiness. How? It happens inevitably whenever we drift away from the Lord, allowing the world to define us, deceive us, distract us. It takes constant vigilance!

And sometimes we will see the results.

As a senior in high school, I served on a youth evangelism team for our church. One evening we called on Danny, a cold and totally unreceptive prospect. I'll never forget how he rubbed the ashes from his cigarette into his jeans while we shared with him. He engaged in conversation (or more properly, debate) and made it very clear he saw no need for Jesus. We left with a prayer that we hadn't spoken in vain—but doubted our words had made any impact.

Four years later, a young man walked up to me in church. Although he looked familiar, I couldn't place him. He introduced himself: "Hello, Doug, I'm Danny. You may not remember me, but four years ago you shared the gospel with me. That was the first time I'd ever heard it, and you got me thinking. I accepted Jesus as my Lord and Savior six months ago. I've been praying I'd get to see you to thank you."

We thought we had utterly failed as salt, but God had planted a seed (to mix the metaphors) in what seemed to be the worst possible soil. And God gave the growth! Praise Him!

Be Light in Darkness

Jesus calls us the light of the world to bring hope and clarity in places of worldly darkness.

Darkness manifests itself in multiple life circumstances:

The darkness of ignorance about God and spiritual life
The darkness of hiding from God and truth
The darkness of deception and shadows
The darkness of evil

Most often, darkness is more subtle than a total eclipse. It's more like a fog or smog, where the sun gets obscured by pollution. Our world goes dark in the hurry and worry of life.

Light overcomes the fear of darkness. Light expresses itself in the good works that reveal God's kindness and care for the world.

A teacher assigned to visit children in a large city hospital received a routine call requesting that she visit a particular child. She took down the boy's name and room number, and the student's teacher told her, "We're studying nouns and adverbs in his class now. I'd be grateful if you could help him with his homework, so he doesn't fall behind the others."

When the visiting teacher reached the boy's room, she realized it was located in the hospital's burn unit. No one had prepared her to find a young boy horribly burned and in great pain. But since she felt she couldn't just turn and walk out, she awkwardly stammered, "I'm the hospital teacher and your teacher sent me to help you with nouns and adverbs."

The next morning a nurse on the burn unit asked her, "What did you do to that boy?" Before she could utter an avalanche of apologies, the nurse interrupted: "You don't understand. We've been very worried about him; but ever since you were here yesterday, his whole attitude has changed. He's fighting back, responding to treatment... It's as though he's decided to live."

The boy later explained that he had completely given up hope until he saw that teacher. Everything changed when he came to one simple realization. With joyful tears he expressed it this way: "They wouldn't send a teacher to work on nouns and adverbs with a dying boy, would they?"[52]

Faith in God is not about religious activity! Religious activity has a place, of course, such as in worship, study, small groups, church leadership, and ministry opportunities. But we must never allow these to crowd out the common acts of kindness and care that come with being good neighbors, good citizens, and good people.

Shine the light of love into people's lives and watch what happens!

20
Identity Sets Healthy Boundaries

Your identity in Christ enables you to stand strong as an individual in Christ.

As leaders, too often we overstep our responsibility for both people and projects. We need a healthy sense of self-definition. We must remind ourselves that we are responsible *to*, not *for*, people. We must learn to resist our tendency to take responsibility *from* people, which is the dynamic of rescuing, characteristic of codependency.

People mature through responsibility and failure. When Paul teaches Christians that the ministry belongs to *all* God's people (Ephesians 4:11-12), he also teaches them the reason: "From him the whole body, joined and held together by every supporting ligament, grows and builds itself up in love, *as each part does its work*" (Ephesians 4:16, NIV, emphasis added).

I do not use the term "volunteer" in the context of church life. *All* Jesus' followers are called to ministry, not just a privileged few who have a particular calling as pastors or ministry leaders. I prefer the word "partners." Volunteers ask, "Will I take part in the work?" while partners ask, "What part of the work will I take?"

In family systems theory, this characteristic of healthy self-definition is called differentiation:

> Differentiation is the capacity to define and maintain your own vision, mission, values and life goals apart from the surrounding "togetherness" pressures, to say "I" when others are demanding "you" [the blaming "you"] or "we."[53]

In the classic book *Boundaries: When to Say Yes, When to Say No to Take Control of Your Life*, Henry Cloud and John Townsend write about differentiation in terms of boundaries:

> A boundary shows me where I end and someone else begins … Any confusion of responsibility and ownership in our lives is a problem of boundaries. Just as homeowners set a physical

property line around their land, so we need to set mental, physical, emotional, and spiritual boundaries for our lives to help us distinguish what is our responsibility and what isn't.[54]

Paul's counsel to the Galatians makes an important distinction that helps us understand the need to respond to others, but to be responsible only for ourselves. He distinguishes between the load that is our responsibility to carry and the burden that exceeds our load.

> Brothers and sisters, if someone is caught in a sin, you who live by the Spirit should restore that person gently. But watch yourselves, or you also may be tempted. Carry each other's burdens, and in this way you will fulfill the law of Christ. If anyone thinks they are something when they are not, they deceive themselves. Each one should test their own actions. Then they can take pride in themselves alone, without comparing themselves to someone else, for each one should carry their own load (Galatians 6:1-5, NIV).

An important distinction exists between a "load" and a "burden." Each one of us has a legitimate load of responsibilities that we must carry. But we also have burdens that we bear with the help of others, even as we help them with their burdens.

Leaders do not ignore human needs and concerns, but they are not driven by pleasing others (Galatians 1:10). Leaders continually remind themselves that they are responsible *to* others, but they are not responsible *for* them. Everyone is ultimately responsible for themselves alone. Above all, leaders keep their eyes on the Lord as they serve others.

It can be difficult to know what to do when someone we care about is going through a challenging time. You might think this advice seems selfish, but if we consider the science behind it, you might discover that the healthiest plan is to take care of yourself first. Such a decision involves self-differentiation.

As noted, differentiation is the capacity to define and maintain your own vision, mission, values, and life goals – in other words, your identity—in the midst of pressures to take on the identities, expectations, and responsibilities others want to impose on you.

Murray Bowen first introduced the term self-differentiation; his ideas became the basis of family systems therapy. Self-differentiation has two aspects: intrapsychic differentiation and interpersonal differentiation. Intrapsychic differentiation refers to the ability to distinguish our thoughts from our emotions—self-awareness, in other words. By contrast, interpersonal differentiation refers to the ability to distinguish *our* experience from the experience of those to whom we are connected. Both aspects of self-differentiation are important, as they empower us to remain aware of our current state and the influence of various interactions and environments on our state so we can take action.[55]

Leaders are often motivated by the desire to help others, to improve life for others, to see others thrive. That noble motivation can lead to over-functioning, which occurs when you do too much for others. Over-functioning leads to other's under-functioning. This is the concept of *homeostasis*, in which a system seeks balance or equilibrium.

Consider a mother who values an orderly home who picks up her teenage son's dirty socks to keep his room tidy. The problem is that she's over-functioning, taking responsibility from her son. Her son is under-functioning, neglecting his responsibility as part of the household. How could the mother more appropriately respond? To function normally, she might wash her son's socks only when she finds them in the hamper. When he complains he has no socks, she can explain her reasonable expectations. The son may go barefoot or wear shoes without socks for a while, but eventually, the equilibrium will likely reset with his appropriate functioning.

The illustration gets far more interesting and intense when translated to the leader's functioning in business. The pressure can grow when employees or coworkers under-function and so put many at risk. Wise leaders, rooted in their identity in Christ, know that each person *must* (not merely *should*) carry their own load. Leaders who rescue under-functioning workers set up both themselves and their teams for failure. Leaders who expect responsibility and maintain their own appropriate boundaries, however, tend to see their teams respond. Still, at times, that response is for a team member to leave or be terminated.

Jesus let the rich young ruler walk away (Luke 18:18-30). Jesus let Judas make his choices (John 13:21-30). Jesus lets you make your choices.

That's the way of spiritual health and maturity. That's the fruit of knowing who you are and whose you are.

21
Who Is a Leader?

What is your identity as a leader?

Leadership includes a wide variety of situations.[56] Most simply, leaders are those who exercise influence. This influence can be formal (as in a work situation between an employer and employee) or more informal (as in the influences we have on friends, family, and in our various social relationships).

Leaders can be the teacher in front of the classroom or the student to whom other students look for guidance or direction. They can be the supervisor at the manufacturing plant or the worker who brings spark and energy to the workplace. Leaders are parents in the home, neighbors in the community, members of a church, employers and employees in the world of work.

In their ground-breaking book, *Leaders: The Strategies for Taking Charge*, Warren Bennis and Burt Nanus assert that "Decades of academic analysis have given us more than 350 definitions of leadership."[57] While they don't document their assertion, few would question it. In fact, I'm sure the number has increased significantly since their book's publication.

Leadership can be described in terms similar to how Charles Hodge[58] described the gospel: "The gospel is so simple that small children can understand it, and it is so profound that studies by the wisest theologians will never exhaust its riches." Likewise, we know leadership when we see it, but we cannot exhaust the depths of its complexities and dynamics.

The "typical" leader can feel overwhelmed with the challenges he or she faces. Lifelong learning and coaching are essential. But unless that learning and coaching are rooted in a life founded on eternal truth in Christ, leaders will be "tossed to and fro" by the waves of human pressures and the relentless crush of information and theory. Unless they learn to lead from the inside out, they will flounder. This is why I believe that leaders benefit not only from IQ and EQ[59] but most importantly from the person's SQ—spirituality quotient.[60] In other words, the combination of your intelligence, your interpersonal skills, and your self-management/soul-management—all framed in the context of your infinite worth in Christ and your eternal purpose—form the foundation for the most effective and satisfying experience of life and leadership.

Good Leadership Is Not Automatic

Dr. J. Robert (Bobby) Clinton, Professor at Fuller Theological Seminary in the School of World Mission (or Intercultural Studies), specialized in leadership studies. One of Professor Clinton's most unsettling conclusions in his research on leadership is that few leaders finish well.[61] "Thirteen of forty-nine Bible leaders who had material indicating their finish, finished well." But if we don't finish well, how will people judge the initial phases of our life's work? A negative ending casts a long, dark shadow over an entire lifetime.

Think of King David. His adultery with Bathsheba and his arrangement for the murder of Uriah, Bathsheba's husband, meant "the sword would never depart from [his] house" (2 Samuel 12:10). God forgave David's sins, but He did not erase their consequences.

We might have hoped that King Solomon, David's son, would have learned from his father's experience. But Solomon, whose reign exhibited a glory never seen before nor since in Israel, finished very poorly:

> And the LORD was angry with Solomon, because his heart had turned away from the LORD, the God of Israel, who had appeared to him twice and had commanded him concerning this thing, that he should not go after other gods. But he did not keep what the LORD commanded. Therefore the LORD said to Solomon, "Since this has been your practice and you have not kept my covenant and my statutes that I have commanded you, I will surely tear the kingdom from you and will give it to your servant. Yet for the sake of David your father I will not do it in your days, but I will tear it out of the hand of your son. However, I will not tear away all the kingdom, but I will give one tribe to your son, for the sake of David my servant and for the sake of Jerusalem that I have chosen" (1 Kings 11:9-13, ESV).

Leaders cannot coast. Those who rest on their laurels will find they have a very small bed.[62]

As Daniel Goleman and many others explain, leaders cultivate knowledge, attitudes, behaviors, and skills in the areas of self-awareness and self-management, as well as in social awareness and relationship management.[63] But the fundamental need is for an identity independent from your leadership role and performance. An identity received in Christ, not achieved and perpetuated by your own efforts. That God-given identity will stand the tests that both life and time will bring.

22
Your Identity Will Be Tested

This section (Part Two) opened with three quotes from the Gospels concerning Jesus' identity.

In the first quote, God the Father clearly acknowledged Jesus as His Son at Jesus' baptism: "the Holy Spirit descended on him in bodily form like a dove. And a voice came from heaven: 'You are my Son, whom I love; with you I am well pleased'" (Luke 3:22, NIV).

Following His baptism, God's Spirit led Jesus into the wilderness. This was a profound period of forty days when (we surmise) Jesus entered into deep silence and solitude to discern God's plan for His ministry. It's fascinating that the primary message of the Gospels regarding this time is that Jesus was "tested." More specifically, Jesus' publicly acknowledged *identity* was tested:

> The devil said to Jesus, "*If* you are the Son of God, tell this stone to become bread."
>
> Jesus answered, "It is written: 'Man shall not live on bread alone'" (Luke 4:3-4 NIV).

> The devil led Jesus to Jerusalem and had him stand on the highest point of the temple. "*If* you are the Son of God," he said, "throw yourself down from here… Jesus answered, "It is said: 'Do not put the Lord your God to the test." (Luke 4:9, 12, NIV).

The devil's strategy aimed to challenge Jesus' identity, to undermine Jesus' confidence, and to influence Jesus' ministry strategy. Turning stones into bread would gain a following, for sure—so long as the bread lasted. A spectacular dive from the temple, resulting in a miraculous soft landing, would capture people's attention and admiration—temporarily (though the evidence of the Gospels declares that miracles had only modest results in convincing people of Jesus' true identity).

In his excellent book *Building a Discipling Culture*, Mike Breen frames these three temptations in terms of Approval, Appetite, and

Ambition.[64] Each of the three are central aspects of being human. "In the beginning," writes Breen, "when the world was still young, the Lord looked upon the crown of his creation—the first man and the first woman—and did three things: he gave them his Approval, he satisfied their Appetite, and he defined their Ambition."[65]

Since the "fall" (Genesis 3), when humanity rejected God's sovereign love and rule, we have tried to satisfy these needs in our own power. Left unchecked, these drives can overwhelm us.

Pursuing Ambition, we end up realizing that we can never *do* enough to bring ultimate satisfaction. Seeking Approval, we realize we will never *be* enough to feel worthy beyond the shadow of a doubt. Trying to satisfy our Appetites leaves us frustrated because we will never *have* enough to fill our voracious need. Leaders need to be aware that these dynamics are also at work in those we lead and serve.

Which need tends to drive *you*?

Jesus faced each test, exposing the deception and rebuking Satan by the truth and power of God's Word. The result? Jesus emerged from the testing with power—*dunamis*.

That power was the foundation of His authority.

23
Authority: The Force of Presence, Not the Presence of Force

Your authority as a leader is ultimately rooted in your person, not in your position. Others are most impressed by who you are, not the position you hold.

I usually say that credentials have a shelf-life of sixty to ninety seconds, once people meet you. Most of us can sense "phony" or "authentic" with just a few moments of interaction. If you've had the experience of finally meeting a person you've admired and appreciated, only to have them barely acknowledge you as they look over and around you to see who else is in the room, you know what I mean.

Many years ago, my friend, H. Spees, then Area Director of Youth for Christ for Fresno California, was speaking to a Rotary meeting about his family's decision to relocate from the suburbs to a house in downtown Fresno. When asked why he would do such a thing, he explained that he had been learning a great deal about power. He said he'd come to the realization that power comes from sources we often fail to appreciate. Then he told the following story:

> Back in the late 1960s or early 1970s, a man visited Harvard to speak to the students and faculty. As he stepped onto the stage, the students booed and hissed and jeered and heckled him so much that he wasn't able to speak. He was surrounded by all the symbols of power. There were secret service agents. There was a briefcase with the ability to start a nuclear war—and yet President Richard Nixon could not gain the attention of the students for a single second. He was driven from the stage.

> Several years later, students and faculty of Harvard University gathered in that same auditorium when a little old woman walked to the middle of the stage. According to the *John Harvard's Journal* of July-August, 1982:

> She spoke strongly against abortion and premarital sex, and in favor of prayer... "Virginity is the most beautiful gift a young

man and young woman can give each other. Make a resolution that on your wedding night you will give each other something beautiful." But she said, "If a mistake has been made, have the courage to accept the child. Do not destroy it. That sin is murder.'" And so, Mother Theresa spoke to a hushed, totally attentive audience. When she finished, she was given a standing ovation.[66]

What made the difference in the students' reaction? We might say it was an issue of power. The students understood the awesome power of a person who comes alongside the least and gives them her best. Her presence exuded both credibility and power that nothing else could replace.

So, how long does such authority last? How long does your identity endure beyond your specific leadership roles and responsibilities? Let's look at that next.

24
Retirement Does Not Change Your Identity

Retirement may seem a long way off for you, but it often factors into one's thinking and planning long before it actually happens. Most people plan extensively in terms of their finances, something both wise and necessary. But most fail to plan for the emotional, spiritual, mental, and relational aspects of retirement.

How will *you* think about *your* identity and worth in retirement? Will you refer back to what you used to do? "I'm a retired teacher," or "executive," or "accountant," or "law enforcement officer…" Or will you tell yourself that you are the same person the day before you retire and the day after you retire? It's just that you have a different schedule and different source of income following the completion of your active work life.

This does not minimize the adjustments we need to make when we retire! Retirement removes the props of position. One retired executive reported the painful realization that "In just six months I went from 'Who's Who,' to 'Who's He?'"[67] It's sobering to realize how quickly people, groups, and organizations move on. But to survive and thrive, they must do exactly that.

I define retirement like this: "Retirement is releasing the burdensome responsibilities of a career so that you can focus on your ultimate contribution."

Bobby Clinton defines an ultimate contribution as "a lasting legacy of a Christian worker for which he or she is remembered, and which furthers the cause of Christianity" (we will explore this concept more fully under Part Three: Destiny). I believe this concept applies to everyone—not only to Christian workers.

I think of our ultimate contribution as the gift we love to give. It may or may not be part of how we have earned our living. But it is what helps make life worth living. Many of us "retire" from a particular career but never stop working. We usually move on to something closer to our "sweet spot" of doing what we really love.

In my own life, I retired three years later than the Social Security-based retirement age at the time. Then I immediately formed a not-for-profit organization, Lorica Ministries, through which I could continue to minister in the areas of my lifelong calling and passion.[68] While I genuinely miss the impact and involvement I had in pastoral ministry, I'm grateful now to be able to focus on more specific projects at a more manageable pace. Regardless of my age, my identity is based on who I am in Christ, not on what position I hold.

25
Sail Confidently in Your Christ-Centered Identity

It's time to put all this together by contrasting rowing and sailing. A Rowing-Identity is driven by the seductive voices of the world. It's all about the effort we exert and the rewards we seek. We keep one eye on the task and one eye on the important people watching, whom we want and need to impress. We often work excessive hours, usually at the cost of personal and family time, to advance our position and status. We postpone pleasures and commitments *now* in the hope of enjoying rich rewards *later*.

But sometimes those who have been part of our lives get tired of waiting for that "just-around-the-corner" moment that never seems to arrive. The near-term love and joy of life get poured out on the altar of self-centered ambition, often disguised as "sacrifice" for others who openly tell us they want *us*, not our "sacrifice." The blisters on our hands and the ache in our arms only magnify the futility of self-reliance.

A Sailing-Identity, by contrast, is received and savored moment by moment. We know we are children of God created to be salt and light in God's world. We care deeply about being faithful to our work. We remain committed to leading with confidence and integrity. We appreciate the rewards and benefits that may come but we know we ultimately serve one Lord. We live free from the expectations that previously shackled us. We see through the deceptions that once baited us. And we refuse to be distracted by the shiny things that once captivated our attention. And through it all, we put up our sails to rely on God's power, to do God's work, God's way, for God's glory.

But how do we capture the bracing wind of the Holy Spirit? Really, it's not as hard as you might expect.

26
Spiritual Disciplines Keep Your Inner Game of Identity Alive

As noted in Part One, spiritual exercises both strengthen and focus our souls. Through them we catch the wind of the Spirit and sail forward in God's power.

Too often we allow our inner world to get neglected or eclipsed by the immediate demands and clamoring voices of the outside world. Two primary clusters of disciplines help us support and maintain our identity in Christ.

The first cluster includes *Disciplines of Perspective: Renewing our Minds.*[69] Our thinking determines our self-perception. The King James Version of Proverbs 23:7 says, "For as [a person] thinketh in his heart, so is he." Since we are "transformed by the renewing our minds" (Romans 12:2), that's the starting point for owning our new identity in Christ.

Consider a few of the primary texts that define our worth. You would be wise to rivet your attention and hold fast to these powerful statements of your identity.

- By faith in Jesus Christ, I am a child of God.
    - » But to all who did receive him, who believed in his name, he gave the right to become children of God (John 1:12, ESV).
    - » For all who are led by the Spirit of God are children of God. So you have not received a spirit that makes you fearful slaves. Instead, you received God's Spirit when he adopted you as his own children. Now we call him, "Abba, Father" (Romans 8:14-15, NLT).
- I am alive *now* as part of God's plan.
    - » For you formed my inward parts;
      you knitted me together in my mother's womb...
      Your eyes saw my unformed substance;
      in your book were written, every one of them,

> the days that were formed for me,
> when as yet there was none of them (Psalm 139:13, 16).

> » For we are his workmanship, created in Christ Jesus
> for good works, which God prepared beforehand, that
> we should walk in them (Ephesians 2:10, ESV).

In a world like ours that is actively hostile or passively indifferent to the Lord, we need to read and study God's Word regularly, even daily. That's essential for our spiritual recalibration. The Scriptures you read throughout this book deserve more than a passing glance. Take the time to journal your reflections on passages that capture your attention.

The second cluster includes *Disciplines of Power: Fasting, Silence, and Solitude*.[70] Jesus practiced these disciplines when Satan challenged his identity in the wilderness. Allow me to give a bit more context for these less familiar disciplines.

Christians have always found themselves caught in the tension of being spiritual in a material world. God created all things good. We have bodies and legitimate physical needs and desires. "For everything God created is good, and nothing is to be rejected if it is received with thanksgiving, because it is consecrated by the word of God and prayer" (1 Timothy 4:4, ESV).

Nevertheless, we, along with the world, have been "infected by sin," so that the things of the world can distract us from God and lead us into sin and away from God.

Many Christians throughout the centuries, therefore, have practiced ascetic disciplines to temper their relationship with the world. The word "ascetic" comes from the Greek *askesis*, usually translated "discipline" or "training." In a Christian context, it usually means the disciplines of depravation, such as fasting, silence, solitude, poverty, and chastity.

The image behind the term "ascetic" is being an athlete for God, getting in shape through diligent training. As Paul writes,

> Do you not know that in a race all the runners run, but only one gets the prize? Run in such a way as to get the prize. Everyone who competes in the games goes into strict training. They do it to get a crown that will not last, but we do it to get a crown that will last forever. Therefore, I do not run like someone running aimlessly; I do not fight like a boxer beating the air. No, I strike a blow to my body and make it my slave so that after I

have preached to others, I myself will not be disqualified for the prize (1 Corinthians 9:24-27, ESV).

Christians recognize the problems that arise when we use life's comforts to avoid God. So, it makes sense that we can use *dis*comfort to become more aware and attentive to God. As the Christian faith spread in the early centuries, those who sought a fuller experience of Christ through intentional discipline developed certain practices.

As noted, Jesus himself modeled a pattern of spiritual discipline that included fasting, silence, and solitude (Luke 4:1-14). The basis for considering these as disciplines of power comes from the fact that Jesus returned from the wilderness in the power (*dunamis*) of the Holy Spirit.

So then, how can such disciplines help a leader immersed in the demands of business? For one thing, they become vivid reminders of what really matters. These disciplines detach us from our worldly power so that we attach to God's power. They are also disciplines for freedom.

Many people often view these disciplines (fasting, solitude, silence) in negative terms, especially in terms of deprivation. The positive application of these disciplines comes to light when we realize that the essence of the disciplines is, in fact, freedom.

While solitude requires the deprivation of relationships, it also is a way to break the power of peer pressure and people-pleasing.

While silence is deprivation of speech, it also can break the power of words that manipulate, curse, and self-justify.

Fasting means deprivation of food, but it also is a way to break the control of bodily appetites.

That's a strange way of looking at it, you might think. But in our confused age we often have mistakenly defined freedom as the ability to do whatever we want, whenever we want. In fact, that's a seductive distortion of freedom. You do not find freedom in eating all the food you want, whenever you want. Freedom comes in restraining your appetite so that you can do with or without food, in arriving at a place where food doesn't control you.

You don't find freedom by experiencing any pleasure you want, whenever you want. You gain real freedom by controlling yourself so that you can savor appropriate pleasures without them exercising control over you.

"I know how to be abased," wrote the apostle Paul, "and I know how to abound; in any and all circumstances, I have learned the secret of facing plenty and hunger, abundance and want. I can do all things in him who strengthens me" (Philippians 4:12,13, ESV).

Now, *that's* freedom!

I encourage you to take some time to choose one discipline among the two clusters listed above that will help you most at this time to more firmly root and cultivate your identity in Christ. Don't try to do more than one! That could overwhelm you. Practicing one consistently, such as reading the Bible five minutes a day, or one chapter a day, will have more impact over time than a quick burst of doing many that just as quickly fades.

Now that you can better respond to the question, "Who am I?" you're better equipped to consider, "Why am I here and where am I going?"

Part Three

Destiny: Pursue Your Ultimate Purpose

*Jesus, knowing that the Father had given all things into his hands,
and that he ... was going back to God ...*

—JOHN 13:3 (ESV)

Once we start with who, then we're ready for the Why. That's the subject of this section.

Knowing our destiny gives us the motivation that fuels our ultimate purpose. Leaders who focus on the ultimate Why understand that they live for the long game of life beyond this one. They have a different perspective, a different set of values, and a different way of living in this world.

Leaders who live from purpose interpret everything that happens to them—from success to suffering and all in between—in the light of eternal life. This glorious reality shapes their ultimate legacy, one that lasts.

We are alone. Everything is gratuitous, this garden, this city and myself. When you suddenly realize it, it makes you feel sick and everything begins to drift…that's nausea.

—JEAN PAUL SARTRE'S AUTOBIOGRAPHY, *NAUSEA*, 1938

"My name is Ozymandias, King of Kings;
Look on my Works, ye Mighty, and despair!"
Nothing beside remains. Round the decay
Of that colossal Wreck, boundless and bare
The lone and level sands stretch far away.

—PERCY BYSSHE SHELLEY, *OZYMANDIAS* (ALT)

Mr. Holland had a profound effect on my life, and on a lot of lives, I suspect. And yet I get the feeling he considers a great part of his own life misspent. Rumor has it he was always working on this symphony of his that would make him rich and famous. But he isn't rich, and he isn't famous, at least not outside our little town.

So, it might be easy for him to think himself a failure. But he would be wrong. Because he's achieved a success far beyond riches and fame. Look around you. There is not a life in this room you have not touched. And each of us is a better person because of you. We are your symphony, Mr. Holland. We are the melodies and the notes of your opus, and we are the music of your life.

—GERTRUDE LANG, GOVERNOR
(FORMER STRUGGLING CLARINETIST).
MR. HOLLAND'S OPUS[71]

27
Futility Is Real in This Fallen World

To understand the element of destiny central to a leader's spiritual vitality, we must first acknowledge the reality of futility and even absurdity that characterize life in this world. Problems, obstacles, and disappointments threaten to smother the hope that fuels destiny. Many who have enjoyed great success often find themselves utterly disillusioned in the middle of it.

The words of the Preacher of Ecclesiastes (traditionally acknowledged as King Solomon, David's son) ring true to all of us at some point:

The words of the Preacher, the son of David, king in Jerusalem.

"Vanity of vanities," says the Preacher;
"Vanity of vanities, all is vanity."

What profit has a man from all his labor
In which he toils under the sun?" (Ecclesiastes 1:1-3, NKJV).

These words come from the pen of the wealthiest king who ever ruled the twelve tribes of Israel. The great King Solomon served as the developer for the most significant, extensive, and expensive building projects in Israel's history. His greatest construction project was the temple, long planned-for and provided-for by his father, King David. Solomon accumulated vast riches, enjoyed the finest pleasures the world had to offer, wielded international influence and prestige, and was given wisdom second to none. And how did he assess life "under the sun"? "Vanity of vanities," he sighed, "all is vanity."

The Hebrew word *hebel* ("vanities") includes a variety of provocative nuances which cause us to pause and consider.[72] These include the concept of brevity and unsubstantiality, like the emptiness of the vapor you exhale outside on a cold day. It also means unreliability in the sense of frailty, like leaning for support on a stick that collapses under your weight. Other Bible versions use words like "meaningless" (NLT and NIV) or "smoke" (*The Message*) to render the term *hebel*:

Smoke, nothing but smoke. (That's what the Quester says.)
There's nothing to anything—it's all smoke.

Philosopher Jean Paul Sartre echoed these observations of
Ecclesiastes. He used the term "nausea" to describe his existential
awareness of the stark reality of a life with no purpose beyond the
horizon of this world. His best-known play, *No Exit*, contains the
famous line, "Hell is other people." While Sartre may be an extreme
example, stories of disillusionment can be multiplied.

Percy Bysshe Shelley's poem, *Ozymandias*, makes a dramatic statement on the consequences of illusion-driven striving. Read it slowly
and let its message sink in.

> I met a traveler from an antique land,
> Who said—"Two vast and trunkless legs of stone
> Stand in the desert.... Near them, on the sand,
> Half sunk a shattered visage lies, whose frown,
> And wrinkled lip, and sneer of cold command,
> Tell that its sculptor well those passions read
> Which yet survive, stamped on these lifeless things,
> The hand that mocked them, and the heart that fed;
> And on the pedestal, these words appear:
> My name is Ozymandias, King of Kings;
> Look on my Works, ye Mighty, and despair!
> Nothing beside remains. Round the decay
> Of that colossal Wreck, boundless and bare
> The lone and level sands stretch far away."

Shelley used this classic example of sardonic poetry to portray the
irony of power. This monument, meant as an intimidating testimony
to inspire awe, fear, and subjugation, had crumbled beneath the
persistent forces of wind, sand, and weather. Human power is transitory. In time, the "colossal Wreck, boundless and bare" was all that
remained of the once-imposing might of a long-forgotten king.

It's true, a shadow has cast itself over life. The weariness and wear-
and-tear of living on a fallen planet has eclipsed the sun of optimism.
While we might expect such a sentiment from those who don't believe in
the God of the Bible, or those of a heathen, pagan culture such as King
Ozymandias, it might surprise us to hear it from Solomon. But Scripture
is refreshingly candid. It declares that those who believe in God, even
those who trust in Jesus Christ, can experience the same rude awakening.

Even as Ecclesiastes exposes us to the harsh reality of a life devoted to success in this world, it also proclaims the necessity of seeing every aspect of life in the light of the eternal. Then—and only then—can we gain the perspective and sense of proportion that allow us to appreciate the responsibilities and pleasures of life in this world. We learn that it's not what life brings to us, but what we bring to life, that ultimately matters.

Until we face the reality of futility and death, life will continue to frustrate us. But ironically, once we understand and accept this reality, we can move forward with both purpose and joy. And where do we find those things? We find them by looking beyond the immediate to the big picture.

The cue to our destiny, in fact, is that *really* big picture. To see it, we need long-range—*really* long-range—planning.

28
A Sense of Destiny

Many of us have what I call a "limited" sense of destiny. We have the sense that we are called to make a difference. We want to lead a life that matters beyond merely living for ourselves.

In his book, *A Prayer for Owen Meany*,[73] John Irving presents the fictional story of Owen, whom today we would call a "little person." Irving wrote the novel in 1989 and described Owen like this: "a tiny dwarf, who has weirdly luminous skin and an ethereally nasal voice" (represented in the novel in all-capital letters).

Owen came to believe that he was God's instrument on Earth, and that he was destined to die heroically. While in school, Owen began to make his friend, John, practice something he called "The Shot," a basketball move in which John lifted Owen up for a slam dunk. They performed this maneuver repeatedly—for reasons unclear from the beginning—trying to accomplish it as quickly as possible.

Years after high school, in 1968, Owen began working as a casualty-assistance officer during the Vietnam War, escorting the bodies of dead soldiers back to their families. One day, Owen called John and asked him to meet for a few days in Phoenix, Arizona, where Owen was on assignment. John flew to Phoenix, where he and Owen spent a few days relaxing. John met the bereaved family that Owen was then helping. The family came from a dangerous part of town. John especially noticed the dead soldier's younger brother, a huge, menacing fifteen-year-old named Dick Jarvits, who lived for the day he would be able to join the military so he could exact revenge for his brother's death by slaughtering the Vietnamese.

When John and Owen went to the airport for John's return flight on the day that Owen believed he was destined to die, they saw a group of nuns escorting a column of Vietnamese war orphans through the airport corridors. One nun asked Owen to take the boys to a men's room. Unknown to them, Dick Jarvits was also at the airport and saw the war orphans enter the bathroom. He burst into the bathroom with a grenade and hurled it at John, who tossed it to Owen. Owen jumped into the air, and John held him up so that Owen could throw the grenade into a high window alcove, a move *exactly* like the "The Shot" they had practiced for years. While the move shielded the children from the blast, Owen's arms were blown off and he bled to death.[74]

I've felt like Owen Meany—with a sense of destiny that I would face a crisis and have to make a very hard decision. My pastor and mentor, Jerry Kirk, once said, "Doug, someday you're going to have to take a big risk." When Jerry first said it, a mixture of feelings hit me. At first, I felt judged, as though Jerry was accusing me of playing life too safe. I could point to several risks I had taken. But I also felt a sense anxiety, wondering if I would be up to the more rigorous test Jerry seemed to predict would come my way. And, sure enough, a test did come my way that required me to, quite literally, put my "ministry career" on the line—and, by God's grace and strength, I answered the call.

While it's valid to see our destiny as limited to this world, as we'll see, such a perspective is incomplete. Ecclesiastes makes it clear that a perspective limited to this world will inevitably result in disappointment, or again to use Sartre's term, nausea.

Paul offered the same principle of limited destiny in commenting on Jesus' resurrection: "If only for this life we have hope in Christ, we are of all people most to be pitied" (1 Corinthians 15:19, NIV). We must see everything we do in the light of the resurrection.

Jesus' followers understand their destiny is linked to God's kingdom coming "on earth as it is in heaven." Why do we so often miss the radical implications of this petition? I think we do so because of the way we often articulate this prayer. Most pastors and congregations I know tend to recite the Lord's prayer with the following phrasing:

> Our Father (pause)
> Who art in Heaven (pause)
> Hallowed be Thy name. (pause)
> Thy kingdom come (pause)
> Thy will be done (pause)
> On earth as it is in heaven.

The pause after "Thy will be done" troubles me the most. I believe that pause indicates a gap in pursuing our kingdom calling. For the sake of both comprehension and application, we should instead recite the Lord's Prayer in complete, unbroken sentences, like this:

Our Father who art in heaven, hallowed be thy name.
Thy Kingdom come, *thy will be done on earth* as it is in heaven.

Our destiny is to live as agents of God's coming kingdom. We must be devoted to pursuing God's will on earth, mirroring the complete expression of God's will in heaven. We are not simply marking time while we await Jesus' return or the coming of the new heavens and new earth. What we do *now* matters. Jesus' coming signaled the in-breaking of God's redemptive initiative to take back his creation from the forces of sin, death, and darkness.

What we do now has eternal implications. "So, my dear brothers and sisters, be strong and immovable. Always work enthusiastically for the Lord, for you know that nothing you do for the Lord is ever useless" (1 Corinthians 15:58, NLT).

Eternal life is not just something in the "sweet by-and-by,"[75] but for the here-and-now.

29
The Foundation for Our Motivation in Life

A leader's soul—*your soul*—is rooted in identity and focused on destiny. Our identity as children of God automatically enrolls us as partners in service to the Kingdom of God. That service fixes our sights on God's will and purpose for our lives.

> Therefore, since we are surrounded by such a great cloud of witnesses, let us throw off everything that hinders and the sin that so easily entangles. And let us run with perseverance the race marked out for us, fixing our eyes on Jesus, the pioneer and perfecter of faith (Hebrews 12: 1-2, NIV).

Our identity defines our meaning and anchors our value. Our destiny fuels our motivation. It directs our daily steps and keeps our attention on our life in Christ, which is abundant and eternal.

Life Abundant

One of Jesus' descriptions for the life he came to give was "abundant" (John 10:10).

I describe the abundant life this way:

Abundant life means "to have life in excess," "life to the fullest extent," "maximum life." Jesus came to give us a quality of life surpassing our wildest expectations in both meaning and satisfaction…

Abundant life is about our quality of life, not a quantity of stuff. It's about becoming a person who lives with confidence, compassion, and an awareness of God's presence. It's an unhurried life. A life of peace amid the storms. A life of generosity, both experienced and shown.[76]

Our destiny in this life is to experience life to the fullest in Christ. We resist temptations, overcome trials, pursue bold visions, and sacrifice personal gain for the sake of others by Christ's power within us. We drink deeply from the water of life, eat heartily of the bread of life, and savor the goodness of God's creation.

At the same time, we are aware that life in this world will be filled with tribulation (John 16:33). While we hope to be comforted and vindicated in this world, we take our ultimate comfort in the promise of eternity.

Life Eternal

Following his great poetic description of the seasons of life in Ecclesiastes 3:1-8, the Preacher says,

> What do workers gain from their toil? I have seen the burden God has laid on the human race. He has made everything beautiful in its time. *He has also set eternity in the human heart*; yet no one can fathom what God has done from beginning to end. I know that there is nothing better for people than to be happy and to do good while they live. That each of them may eat and drink and find satisfaction in all their toil—this is the gift of God. I know that everything God does will endure forever; nothing can be added to it and nothing taken from it. God does it so that people will fear him (Ecclesiastes 3:9-14, NIV, emphasis added).

As much as I would love to dig deeply into this passage, let me simply invite you to read it again while noticing two basic themes.

First, we live in the holy tension between time and eternity. That means we always live in a state of frustration because of sin and its consequences. Disease plagues life, betrayal poisons relationships, problems sabotage progress, and so on, so long as sin reigns on this planet. As a result, we must learn to dial back our idealism a bit. We adjust our expectations. We manage our emotional investments. We maintain appropriate boundaries.

Second, the eternal perspective motivates us to invest ourselves *fully* in the work God has called us to do *now* because we know it has eternal implications. We do not give in to despair. We do not give up. We do not lose heart when disappointed in some outcome. We do not depend on worldly signs of success and acceptance. We know God will make all things right.

Therefore we do not lose heart. Though outwardly we are wasting away, yet inwardly we are being renewed day by day. For our light and momentary troubles are achieving for us an eternal glory that far outweighs them all. So we fix our eyes not on what is seen, but on what is unseen, since what is seen is temporary, but what is unseen is eternal (2 Corinthians 4:16-18, NIV).

The eternal reward promised to us in Christ sustains us. The powers of darkness and the consequences of sin have been defeated. We are called to be active in bringing this good news to the world around us.

The sting of death is sin, and the power of sin is the law. But thanks be to God! He gives us the victory through our Lord Jesus Christ. Therefore, my dear brothers and sisters, stand firm. Let nothing move you. Always give yourselves fully to the work of the Lord, because you know that your labor in the Lord is not in vain (1 Corinthians 15:56-58, NIV).

Our destiny beyond this life motivates our choices in this life. *This* determines our Why. We do everything "heartily, as to the Lord and not to men," as it says in the King James version of Colossians 3:23. Consider the full quote:

Whatever you do, work at it with all your heart, as working for the Lord, not for human masters, since you know that you will receive an inheritance from the Lord as a reward. It is the Lord Christ you are serving (Colossians 3:23-24, ESV).

But let's take it a step further. We are not only working for the Lord, but we are also doing the Lord's work, kingdom work. We are continuing Jesus' work in this world.

So, whatever your job may be, approach it as your extension of Jesus' continuing work in this world.

If Jesus himself were doing your job, how would he go about it? That may take some thought! But take the time…it's worth it.

30
The Continuing Incarnation

Several bedrock principles guided me when I served as a non-paid leader with Young Life, a parachurch youth ministry that was a critical part of my early Christian experience. The first principle was "incarnational ministry." I concur with this summary of the principle: "The Young Life approach is to go where teenagers are and care for them, thereby earning 'the right to be heard.'"[77] In a sense, youth workers should see themselves as representatives of God, connecting with teens in the middle of their everyday lives. This is a type of incarnation.

The apostle John may have given us the best description of Jesus' incarnation: "And the Word became flesh (Latin, *carne*) and dwelt among us" (John 1:14, NKJV). John used the term "Word" (Greek *logos*) to designate Jesus. Theologically speaking, Jesus (the Word) took on flesh and entered human experience. The second person of the Holy Trinity became human.

God's strategy is so brilliant it should leave us speechless.

God made him who had no sin to be sin for us, so that in him we might become the righteousness of God (2 Corinthians 5:21, NIV).

Consider how Eugene Peterson phrased this verse in *The Message*:

Become friends with God; he's already a friend with you. How? you ask. In Christ. God put the wrong on him who never did anything wrong, so we could be put right with God.

Incarnational ministry means imitating Jesus' model of entering our context.[78] Jesus came to us instead of insisting that we go to him—because we *couldn't* go to him.

As followers of Jesus, we also follow his method and strategy. Therefore, we go to others; we do not wait for them to come to us.

We enter their lives by being with them, listening to them, caring for them, experiencing life with them.

As a Young Life leader, I visited local high schools at lunchtime to mix with the students. I attended their sports events, plays, and dances. Being incarnational meant being with them on their turf, long before expecting them to come my religious turf.

Leaders often feel tempted to distance or even isolate themselves from employees, followers, and staff. We think we must remain apart from them to ensure a sense of difference and objectivity. But we do not learn this from Jesus! We will discuss this more fully in Part Four on Partnership, but for now, the point is to realize that we follow as closely as possible, in everything we do, the model of Jesus' incarnation.

Something very special happens when we come alongside people. I have always been moved by the story Rebecca Manley Pippert told about a student, Bill, who had come to faith in Christ and looked to be every bit a hippie. He decided to attend a middle-class church across the street from the campus, one filled with well-dressed members. When Bill began walking down the aisle looking for a seat, it seemed as if everyone was watching. On a very crowded Sunday morning as he reached the front pew, he realized that there were no seats. So, Bill just sat down on the carpet. The tension in the air became thick. Becky describes what happened next:

> Suddenly an elderly man began walking down the aisle toward the boy. Was he going to scold Bill? My friends who saw him approaching said they thought, *You can't blame him. He'd never guess Bill as a Christian. And his world is too distant from Bill's to understand. You can't blame him for what he's going to do.*
>
> As the man kept walking slowly down the aisle, the church became utterly silent, all eyes focused on him. You could not hear anyone breathe. When the man reached Bill, with some difficulty he lowered himself and sat down next to him on the carpet. He and Bill worshiped together on the floor that Sunday. I was told there was not a dry eye in the congregation.[79]

No words describe the impact of the elderly man's leadership that day. He went to Bill and just sat down with him—and in so doing transformed a whole congregation.

31
Living in Exile: Be Heavenly-Minded and Earthly Good

The concept of incarnation determines our strategy, while the concept of exile helps us understand our context. The biblical theme of exile provides another useful metaphor for understanding our earthly destiny and purpose in this world.

The historical exile of the Jews took place when they were deported to Babylon following their defeat at the hands of King Nebuchadnezzar in 586 BC.[80] Nebuchadnezzar destroyed the city of Jerusalem, tore down the temple Solomon had built, and took into captivity a huge number of Israelites.

Suddenly, the Jewish people had no temple for their sacrifices. Their captors transported them hundreds of miles from their homeland, mixing them in with the very non-Jewish Babylonians. The exiles no longer enjoyed the protection provided by living in a nation that (at least theoretically) practiced their values and rituals. They were forcibly immersed into a new situation we would call "pluralistic." How would they survive?

We might expect that they would take a defensive posture and isolate themselves from their neighbors. But in a letter to the exiles, the Lord spoke through Jeremiah:

This is the Message from God-of-the-Angel-Armies, Israel's God, to all the exiles I've taken from Jerusalem to Babylon:

"Build houses and make yourselves at home. Put in gardens and eat what grows in that country. Marry and have children. Encourage your children to marry and have children so that you'll thrive in that country and not waste away. Make yourselves at home there and work for the country's welfare. Pray for Babylon's well-being. If things go well for Babylon, things will go well for you" (Jeremiah 29:4-7, *The Message*).

Ponder that command for a moment! God said, "Seek the peace and prosperity of the city to which I have carried you into exile" (Jeremiah 29:7, NIV).

What? Seek the peace and prosperity of a brutal, ungodly city? Seek the welfare of a metropolis filled with oppressors? Strange as it may seem, this is God's strategy for exilic living … which is where we find ourselves, too.

We identify with the author of Hebrews who speaks about believers living as "foreigners and strangers on earth." We are exiles on earth. In the great "Hall of Faith" chapter, the author describes the motivation—the Why—God's people had for living by faith:

> All these people were still living by faith when they died. They did not receive the things promised; they only saw them and welcomed them from a distance, admitting that they were foreigners and strangers on earth. People who say such things show that they are looking for a country of their own. If they had been thinking of the country they had left, they would have had opportunity to return. Instead, they were longing for a better country—a heavenly one. Therefore, God is not ashamed to be called their God, for he has prepared a city for them (Hebrews 11:13-16, NIV).

We live differently when we identify ourselves as exiles, sojourners, pilgrims, resident aliens. What does it look like to identify personally in that way?

We Persistently Focus on God's Kingdom

As Jesus' followers, we surrender our agenda for God's agenda. Certainly, we may still actively pursue a career achievement or a promising business opportunity; but our goal, always, is to use these to further God's kingdom. We exercise holy imagination to see how we might use the resources generated to serve God's work.

In his book, *Gospel Patrons: People Whose Generosity Changed the World*,[81] John Rinehart tells stories from the lives of William Tyndale (the first to translate the New Testament into English), George Whitefield (the British evangelist of the 1700s) and former-slave trader turned Christian John Newton (who wrote the cherished hymn, *Amazing Grace*):

They were the great evangelists, the mouthpieces, who played a critical role in the extraordinary revivals of their time. But what I did not know was that their impact was made possible only because God chose to use three successful businesspeople to collaborate with [and fund] them.

In the final section of this book, I'll tell one of these stories (Lady Huntingdon's home events with Whitefield)[82], but for now, it's important to get the point that throughout history, God has called on people with resources to come alongside God's servants to pursue kingdom impact.

We Define Success Differently

A second aspect of exilic living is that our values shift from an earthly to an eternal timeline. This world is not our ultimate home. We therefore develop what I call a sense of proportion.

Proportion has to do with relative size and significance. A toy car is small and far less significant in proportion to a real car. A doll bears little resemblance to the value and substance of a living human being. Worldly existence pales in proportion to eternal life.

We define success, therefore, in terms of our ultimate destination. This does not mean we don't care about successful achievements in this world, but that we measure them in proportion to eternity. Success means faithfulness, not the accumulation of assets. Success means influence for the Lord, not popularity for us. Success means genuine friendships, not superficial acquaintances.

The parable of the rich fool (see Luke 12:13-21) reminds us that an abundant harvest is worth quite literally nothing when compared to being rich in heavenly treasures. What are heavenly treasures? Jesus clearly teaches in the parable of the sheep and the goats that His heavenly rewards go to those who treat others with care and compassion. "The King will reply, 'Truly I tell you, whatever you did for one of the least of these brothers and sisters of mine, you did for me'" (Matthew 25:40, NIV). This can also translate into treating employees and customers with fairness and generosity.

We Hold Worldly Possessions Loosely

A third implication of exilic living is that we become vividly aware that this world is only our temporary residence. While we value life's pleasures and material blessings, we do not cling to them.

We realize we are more like renters than owners. We have the temporary use of goods and services but do not ultimately possess anything. This is no statement against personal property but rather a recognition of our impermanence in this world.

A strong believer in Christ lost her house and all her earthly goods in The Eaton Fire, the wildfire of January 2025 that devastated Altadena, California (next to Pasadena), destroying more than 9,000 structures and resulting in eighteen fatalities. "People ask me how I can cope with losing everything," she said. "I tell them that I didn't lose everything. I didn't lose my life, and I didn't lose Jesus."

If you were her, could you say the same thing?

32
What's the Real Bottom Line?

Every person in business recognizes the need to pay attention to the bottom line, typically defined as the final measure of success or failure. The bottom line of profit and losses is normally the driving force in corporate vision and decisions.

When I conduct a funeral or memorial service, those attending usually cannot help but reflect on their own life, wondering: *What's the real bottom line in my life? What will matter most to those attending **my** memorial service?* Do these seem like morbid questions? Maybe so, but they put everything else in perspective.

Here's another one: What will matter most to you as you approach your final breath?

"Memento Mori"

Somewhere I read that Alexander the Great, the young Greek general who conquered the then-known world, requested that he be awakened every morning with the words, "Remember that you must die."

The Latin phrase *memento mori*, literally means "*remember that you must die.*" Historical accounts state that this phrase was customarily spoken by a slave to a victorious general returning from battle to prevent him from falling into pride and vain glory (*hubris*).[83]

In light of death, what matters most in life?

When we come to the end of a year, we often do a personal inventory. More poignantly, when thoughtful people gather in the presence of death, they find themselves thinking: What's it all about? or What's the real bottom line?

I'd like to offer three options for the bottom line. These may not be exclusive choices, but one usually dominates a life.

1.   ARE MONEY AND SUCCESS THE REAL BOTTOM LINE?

Many of us define and live our lives pursuing the so-called "American dream" of success, comfort, recognition, and "the good life." These things are fine in and of themselves, but as already noted, untold millions experience the disappointing limits of money and success. Assets don't hold all the answers. We realize, sometimes too late, the downsides of success: the high price it exacts from us, our loved ones, even our health, or the inner discontent that often leaves us disillusioned … that Ecclesiastes feeling.

2.   IS BEING REMEMBERED THE REAL BOTTOM LINE?

Some have a primary goal to establish a legacy that lives on in the memory of those who remain. Again, while this is not an inappropriate goal, it is incomplete. It falls tragically short of God's best for us.

Consider the logic:

- My ultimate goal is to be remembered by those who will also die.
- Ultimately, I will be forgotten.
- Even if my name gets put on a building or a business, nothing lasts forever.

Thankfully, the third possibility for the bottom line is that we were made for something more.

3.   IS OUR DESTINY BEYOND THIS LIFE THE REAL BOTTOM LINE?

We've already noted Ecclesiastes 3:11, which says that God has placed "eternity in our hearts." In a materialistic, rationalistic approach to life, we often ignore and even scoff at such concepts. Yet, the sense of something *more* can haunt us.

Our culture has moved from neutrality regarding spiritual things to total disregard:

> Your neighbors inhabit what Charles Taylor calls an "immanent framework"; they are no longer bothered by "the God question" as a question because they are devotees of "exclusive humanism"– a way of being-in-the-world that offers significance without transcendence. They don't feel like anything is missing.[84]

The German sociologist Max Weber (1864-1920) was the first to call this attitude "disenchantment," referring to the "emancipation of the modern mind from supernaturalism."[85]

But there's a high price for such an emancipation! It cuts us off from all meaning beyond whatever we generate for ourselves. And it fails to address that inner longing that continues to push in on us. Celtic spirituality described this inner longing as the experience of "thin times."

In times such as birth, marriage, death, illness, and personal crisis, we have an instinctive sense that there's more to this life than we can see, more than we often encounter in the normal press of daily living. That thick curtain between time and timelessness gets so thin you can almost see through it; you can feel different stirrings in your heart.

These thin times, these yearning, nagging questions that we often try to push down or push away, are in fact the whispers of God inviting us to enter our eternal purpose. Truly, God *has* placed eternity in our hearts.

Get a Life!

I'm certain you've heard the phrase, "Get a life!" This sarcastic phrase is usually spoken to people who seem to be wasting their lives on trivial, inane pursuits. To people so lost in tiny things that they miss the big things. To people who have their values reversed, giving their energy to things that don't deserve it while ignoring the things that matter most.

But it's also a phrase that describes our ultimate purpose: we are *all* driven to get a life with meaning, with purpose.

A life that satisfies.

So, get a life! What kind of life are you getting now? What kind of life do you want to get? What kind of life *can* you get?

Too many of us settle for mediocrity, for a life of trivial pursuits and questionable purposes, when all along God invites us to enjoy a life filled with joy and satisfaction beyond imagination. God invites us to prioritize the kind of bottom line that sees beyond this life and that transforms how we live.

How would you describe your own bottom line, right now?

33
Our Perspective on Life Matters Ultimately

Contrast Sartre, Ozymandias, and even Solomon in his later disillusionment, with the life and experience of Jim Elliot.[86] Elliot graduated from Wheaton College in 1949 with a call to be a missionary. Two statements in his spiritual journals express his single-hearted loyalty to God. He wrote:

> God, I pray Thee, light these idle sticks of my life, that I may burn for Thee. Consume my life, my God, for it is Thine. I seek not a long life, but a full one, like you, Lord Jesus. (1948)

> One treasure, a single eye, and a sole Master! (1948)

Following graduation, Jim received some training in Bible translation with Wycliffe Bible Translators, where he learned about Ecuador's Quechua people, also called the Waorani. This group of indigenous Ecuadorian people were considered so violent and dangerous to outsiders that they were initially known as the "Auca," the pejorative Quechua word for "savage."

Elliot prayed and planned for six years to prepare for his mission. Then, in 1952, he arrived in Ecuador with the purpose of evangelizing the Waorani people. He and his fellow missionaries (Ed McCully, Roger Youderian, Pete Fleming, and their pilot, Nate Saint) first stayed in Quito and then moved to the jungle. At the age of twenty-eight, Elliot's dream was realized: He took a Waorani by the hand.

Two days later, on Sunday, January 8, 1956, the men for whom Jim Elliott had prayed for six years killed him and his four companions.

Another quote from Jim's journal has served as his epitaph ever since: "He is no fool who gives what he cannot keep to gain that which he cannot lose." Jim Elliot's identity as a child of God gave him confidence to pursue his ultimate destiny, even if it meant a short life.

While it's true most leaders will not literally sacrifice their lives as martyrs, they *will* sacrifice a great deal of time, energy, and even relationships for the sake of fulfilling their sense of calling. All of us must examine what we are doing and then ask the key question: Is *this* really worth it?

34
Rooted in Our Identity, Focused on Our Destiny

A leader's soul is rooted in identity and focused on destiny; everything in between is stewardship and partnership.

Our identity is not subject to the vacillations of life's ages and stages. Our identity is received. We were created in God's image and were born again as new creations in Christ at our redemption.

Still, the *expression* of our identity varies from age to age and stage to stage. We move from infancy to adulthood, from receiving care to providing care, from learner to contributor, from dependence to independence, and, yes, eventually back to dependence and finally, death to this mortal existence. Through it all, every moment, we are by faith children of God. Our destiny includes life in this world with an eye on life beyond this world.

This does not mean, however, that we devalue our present life. Too often we wish our lives away, expecting happiness to be just around the corner. Instead, all we find is another corner. I recall a poster advertising the performance of a major-brand sports car. "Happiness is not around the corner," it says; "it *is* the corner."

Really?

The poem "Present Tense" by Jason Lehman describes far too many of us. He begins with the stanza:

It was Spring,
     But it was Summer I wanted,

The warm days,
     And the great outdoors.

The poem continues moving through the seasons of life with the author always wanting to be in the next season. Then he shifts to the seasons/stages of life:

I was a child,
     But it was adulthood I wanted,

The freedom,
And respect.

I was twenty,
But it was thirty I wanted,

To be mature,
And sophisticated.

That same attitude of dissatisfaction with the present overshadowed every stage of life until:

My life was over.
But I never got what I wanted.

The most poignant fact about this poem is not the message, powerful as that is, but rather the age of the messenger. Jason Lehman was fourteen years of age when he wrote "Present Tense." The poem was sent to Abigail Van Buren, who after verifying that the author was indeed "a teenager wise beyond his years," published it in her newspaper column "Dear Abby" on February 14, 1989.[87] Such wisdom at such a young age should cause us to pause and assess our too-often future-focused mindset.

Even in light of eternity, *now* matters most.

35
Get a Life? Or Shape a Life?

Life is not a commodity we can obtain. It is rather a process of shaping what God has entrusted to us.

We play an active role in the formation of our lives. Physical growth is almost automatic, with the basics of our stature and physical characteristics programmed (so to speak) into our genetic composition. But intellectual, emotional, and spiritual maturation require intentional development. Spiritual growth, especially, is not automatic.

God Makes. We Shape.

God created human beings to engage actively in their own development. God wants us to make choices that bring us into partnership with him. The classic biblical text on this idea is Philippians 2:12-13: "Work hard to show the results of your salvation, obeying God with deep reverence and fear. For God is working in you, giving you the desire and the power to do what pleases him" (NLT). Or consider this translation: "continue to work out your salvation with fear and trembling, for it is God who works in you to will and to act in order to fulfill his good purpose" (NIV).

We remain spiritually underdeveloped unless we take responsibility for our own growth.

> While God makes us and shapes us, God also calls us to join actively in shaping our spiritual lives. Like a wise parent, the Lord cultivates our maturity by not doing all the work for us. We play an essential role in forming our life in Christ. God provides the raw material of personhood. We are given the privilege of forming a healthy life from that raw material.[88]

In his bestseller, *Seven Habits of Highly Effective People*, Stephen Covey advises us to "Begin with the end in mind." Begin with the goal and then reverse-engineer your way to the procedural steps that promise to lead to a good result.

I also encourage you to think in terms of The End—meaning The End of your earthly life.

We easily and consistently lose sight of The End. Charles Dickens' classic A *Christmas Carol* presents three primary variations on this theme in his story of the three Christmas ghosts who visit Ebenezer Scrooge.

The Ghost of Christmas Past reminds Scrooge not only of his harsh childhood (getting blamed by his father for his mother dying at Ebenezer's birth), but also of the love he lost because of his short-sighted focus on making his fortune.

The Ghost of Christmas Present reminds Scrooge of the love that can exist despite dire circumstances (as witnessed in the Cratchit family) and the deadly consequences (literally) of withholding generosity; Tiny Tim's life hung in the balance.

In the final revelation, as Scrooge musters up the courage to view the tombstone to which the Ghost of Christmas Future pointed, he cries out, "Spirit! Hear me! I am not the man I was. I will not be the man I must have been but for this visitation. Why show me this if I am past hope? Assure me that I yet may change these shadows you have shown me, by an altered life!"[89]

One of the final scenes in the 1951 film version of Dickens' tale, starring Alistair Sim, gets me every time. Scrooge has repented by this point, but Bob Cratchit doesn't yet know it. Cratchit comes in late, and Scrooge summons him to his office, apparently as surly as ever. He tells Bob he "won't put up with this" any longer, and then says, "You leave me no alternative … But to raise your salary."

Cratchit stands there, dumbfounded, and Scrooge drops the pretense. He sends Bob out to get another coal scuttle. As Bob leaves, Scrooge says, with his surly voice and face, "I don't deserve to be so happy." But then a wide grin breaks across his face as he adds, "But I can't help it. I just can't help it," and he tosses his pen over his shoulder as he laughs with great delight. That's the joy that comes from true repentance and the transformed life that results from salvation.

While no Christmas ghosts may haunt us, countless visitations rattle our complacency and seek to awaken us from the stupor of our material, world-bound ways. In Christ, we begin with The End in mind. Our ultimate destiny is nothing less than standing and worshiping in the eternal presence of the Triune God who will evaluate our work (Matthew 25, Revelation 7, Hebrews 9).

Pleasing God is our motivation. We live, work, serve, and play to continue Jesus' work in this world. We devote all our energies to being a part of the answer to the prayer, "Thy Kingdom come; thy will be done *on earth as it is in heaven*."

The Lord says to us, "I created you as you; now, do what only you can do."

What kind of life are you getting now?

What kind of life do you want to get?

What kind of life can you get?

Prepare for the Final Audit

The very word "audit" strikes fear in most hearts. It has an ominous ring. By its very nature, it means an accounting, a reckoning, a close examination to determine accuracy and compliance with regulations, laws, and standards of accounting. And there's no getting around it.

Every person, including you and me, will die and stand before the Lord. We must remember daily that we will be called to give an account for our lives. "For we must all appear before the judgment seat of Christ, that each one may receive what is due him, for the things done while in the Body whether good or bad" (2 Corinthians 5:10, NIV). At this time, God will evaluate what we did with His gift of life.

The Bible is clear that *no one* automatically enters heaven. This first stop determines our eternal destiny. This fact alone should cause each of us to halt in our tracks and determine to understand what we must do to ensure that heaven is our final destination.[90]

1.   THE FIRST JUDGMENT: LIFE OR DEATH

When we die, we will appear before the Lord, who will see whether our name is written in the Book of Life (Revelation 20:12). The Book of Life contains the names of those who have put their faith in Jesus Christ. We could think of it as the official roll book of the citizens of heaven.

How does one's name get written in the Book of Life? Your name appears there the moment you put your faith in Jesus Christ as your Lord and Savior. In this first judgment, God will judge people according to their faith in Jesus Christ. If they profess faith in Christ, they will be saved. If they have rejected Christ, they will perish (see John 3:16-17).

2.   THE SECOND JUDGMENT: AN EVALUATION OF FAITHFULNESS AND
     FRUITFULNESS

Believers will immediately pass through the first judgment without a threat. But then they face a second judgment, although it might be more helpful to use the word "evaluation" rather than "judgment."

Those who are in Christ Jesus will never face condemnation (see Romans 8:1); but their work *will* be evaluated. Those who put their faith and trust in Christ, whose names are written in the Book of Life, will be evaluated for what they did with what God gave them.

In Matthew 16:27 (NIV) we read, "The Son of Man is going to come in His father's glory with his angels and then he will reward each person according to what he has done."

Why this evaluation? *Our deeds either confirm or contradict our stated faith commitment.* Even as faithfulness in love confirms a marriage vow, even as integrity in business confirms a contract, so good deeds confirm faith in Jesus Christ.

For some reason, many seem to have lost sight of the importance of living with integrity. Many mistake grace for license, thinking that because we are saved by grace, we need be concerned about nothing else. But Jesus says that true faith will result in a changed life, even as a fruit tree naturally produces fruit (see Matthew 7:15-20). In harmony with the principle that "God makes, we shape," the apostle Paul warns us about paying careful attention to the quality of life we are building:

> For no one can lay any foundation other than the one already laid, which is Jesus Christ. If anyone builds on this foundation using gold, silver, costly stones, wood, hay or straw, their work will be shown for what it is, because the Day will bring it to light. It will be revealed with fire, and the fire will test the quality of each person's work. If what has been built survives, the builder will receive a reward. If it is burned up, the builder will suffer loss but yet will be saved—even though only as one escaping through the flames (1 Corinthians 3:11-15, NIV).

In other words, some of us will arrive in heaven smelling of smoke! Again, this is not about earning salvation through good works, but about revealing our faith and gratitude to God by a life lived to honor God and to continue Christ's work in the world.

36
Discover Your Personal Destiny by Paying Attention

Let's turn now to the consideration of one's destiny in this life. What is your specific role in this life, in light of eternal life?

We can use three related terms to describe our personal destiny: ultimate contribution, vocation, and call.

It's helpful to think of your purpose in life in terms of your ultimate contribution. Dr. J. Robert (Bobby) Clinton, writes:

> An ultimate contribution is a lasting legacy of a Christian worker for which he or she is remembered, and which furthers the cause of Christianity by one or more of the following:
>
> - setting standards for life and ministry,
> - impacting lives by enfolding them in God's kingdom or developing them once in the kingdom,
> - serving as a stimulus for change which betters the world,
> - leaving behind an organization, institution, or movement that will further channel God's work,
> - the discovery of ideas, communication of them, or promotion of them so that they further God's work.[91]

We can also reframe these to describe the ultimate contribution of all Jesus' followers. I would offer this adaptation.

> An ultimate contribution is a Christian's lasting legacy for which he or she is remembered, and which furthers the cause of Christianity by one or more of the following:
>
> - setting standards for life and work consistent with God's Word
> - impacting lives by serving them according to God's standards and seeking to enfold them in God's kingdom or developing them once in the kingdom
> - serving as a stimulus for change which betters the world
> - leaving behind an organization, institution, or movement that will be a witness to Jesus Christ in this world

- the discovery of ideas, communication of them, or promotion of them so that they further God's work and show God's love in practical ways.

A friend is making his ultimate contribution through his business. He teaches all his employees the centrality of the Golden Rule. He tells them, "'Do unto others as you would have them do unto you' is the key to the way we treat each other and our customers. We hope they'll ask, 'What makes you so different?' And then we can tell them the Lord is the ultimate owner of this company."

We can also use the term "vocation" to describe our ultimate contribution. Vocation comes from the Latin word *vocare* (to call). God has issued a call to you to make a unique contribution to His continuing work in this world. Your primary call is to fulfill the design God has woven into your heart. You are to do what you love to show others God's love.

By "vocation" I do not mean simply how you earn a living or how you make money. Your vocation is your primary contribution to life. You might not earn *any* money from your vocation, but you know God wants to give you something that you pass on to others, even if it costs you. I often pray, especially as I write or prepare a message, "Lord, give me what you want me to give others."[92]

Your job may be as a salesperson, for example, but your *vocation* is showing God's love through helping people better understand how to care for themselves. You approach your sales as educational instruction and providing useful resources. Or your career may be a business executive in a large organization; but your *vocation* is funding God's mission in the world. So, you conduct your business in a way that also witnesses to your faith, which may not always be overtly expressed in words but is consistently demonstrated by your professional conduct and respectful interactions.

Bobby Clinton defined our personal destiny this way: "A sense of destiny is an inner conviction arising from an experience or a series of experiences in which there is a growing sense of awareness that God has His hand on a leader in a special way for special purposes."[93]

In biblical terms, we can use the terms "vocation," "call," and "destiny" interchangeably. I suggest the following guidelines for discerning your vocational call, your ultimate contribution.[94]

1. BEGIN EACH DAY AFFIRMING YOUR COMMITMENT TO SERVE
    JESUS.

You could pray, "Lord, may I bring your presence wherever I am, to
whatever I do, and in whatever I say." You will experience a sense of
freedom when you view Jesus as the ultimate "boss" of your work and
other responsibilities.

2. FOCUS ON YOUR BEST OFFERING.

Remember that *how* you do what you do matters as much as *what* you
actually do. There are many things you *could* do but try to determine
what you *must* do—your best contribution. Remind yourself daily to
focus as much as possible on what you sense God has called you to do.

3. PAY ATTENTION TO LIFE-GIVING EXPERIENCES IN YOUR WORK/
    SERVICE SETTING.

Life-giving experiences provide clues to your calling. Review your
work responsibilities to identify the aspects that attract your positive
interest and that generate energy as you do them.

4. PAY ATTENTION TO LIFE-DRAINING EXPERIENCES IN YOUR WORK/
    SERVICE SETTING.

Life-draining experiences also provide clues to your calling (even
though you may have to continue doing some of them) What
responsibilities, tasks, relationships sap your energy? Why? What
steps can you take to better manage them?[95]

37
Sail Consistently into Your Destiny

You can already see that a Rowing-Destiny, determined by your own efforts and limited to your worldly perspective, just won't cut it. It's like playing in mud puddles when you're just a short walk from the ocean. Here's how C. S. Lewis expressed it:

> Our Lord finds our desires, not too strong, but too weak. We are half-hearted creatures, fooling about with drink and sex and ambition when infinite joy is offered us, like an ignorant child who wants to go on making mud pies in a slum because he cannot imagine what is meant by the offer of a holiday at the sea. We are far too easily pleased.[96]

What Could God Do in Your Situation?

Dallas Willard defined discipleship as doing what Jesus would do if he were in your situation. "I am learning from Jesus to live my life as he would live my life if he were I."[97]

What would the Lord like to do with *your* opportunities? How would the Lord like to maximize *your* opportunities? In what ways can the Lord work in the middle of the obstacles and disappointments *you* face?

We unlock great energy and creativity by using holy imagination to pray and to see our lives in fresh ways. A classroom isn't simply a bunch of students. It's a gathering of souls whose welfare matters eternally. So, teachers, pray regularly by name for each student and family. A sales presentation isn't just an opportunity to make a quota; it's an opportunity to care for people living under the stress and pressure of daily life. A staff meeting isn't just an agenda to get through, but a prime time to cultivate a constructive, caring, competent culture.

Destiny expands our lives. We live for a much larger purpose. We don't settle for a small life.

Rowing is about a small life, one limited to our strength and bound by our vision. God wants so much more for you! You are not called to play stereotypes based on a restricted script for your life. God's work in and through you can accomplish more in a moment than you can accomplish on your own in a lifetime.

Take Holy Risks

Don't play it safe. Be wise but know when to call caution an excuse for cowardice.

Commitments drive life. "First we make our commitments, then our commitments make us."[98] Make commitments that stretch you.

One of our family's biggest financial commitments was to a capital campaign at the First Presbyterian Church of Fresno when I served there as lead pastor. We had a goal of raising $1.5 million (a significant amount in the early 1990s) to purchase a city block across the street from the church for parking, and to make some campus improvements.

As we prepared for the campaign, Roy, our consultant, urged me to announce our family's pledge to the campaign in a sermon. I resisted his suggestion for several reasons but agreed to pray about it.

In prayer, Sarah and I came to the point where we felt compelled to double what we initially planned to give. That was a huge step of faith for us because we literally didn't have even 20 percent of the new pledge amount in savings or checking—and we had no idea where the money would come from. With four children in our home at the time from ages ten to sixteen, we lived on a tight budget.

But I also felt that I should make our pledge known publicly. Very soon, the Sunday came for "the sermon." As I neared its close, I said this:

> In spite of my inner resistance to making a sacrificial gift, we can't help but give one. We are overwhelmed by God's faithfulness. All through our lives, Sarah and I have been blessed in wonderful ways: godly parents, a deeply spiritual marriage, a precious family, the special churches that I have served… Above all, there is the priceless gift of knowing Jesus Christ in an ever-deepening way. We are also overwhelmed by you, the people of this congregation. We love this church, and we love you. We have experienced the truth of the proverb: You can't outgive God.
>
> In light of these things, making a sacrifice isn't such a big deal. Therefore, to start off our capital campaign, the Rumford family is grateful to God to pledge $10,000 to be given over the next three years.

You could hear an audible gasp from the congregation. I was in tears and so were many of my listeners. (For a lot of reasons!)

At the door, one man, Wally, said to me, "Doug, I just doubled my pledge." Many made similar remarks on the impact our prayer and commitment made on their decision. The campaign, by God's grace, exceeded its goal in commitments.

But that's just the start of the story!

How would we fulfill our commitment? That question became a matter of daily prayer. About six weeks after announcing our pledge, I received a call from David Mains. I had been working with David's Chicago-based ministry *Chapel of the Air* for two or three years, helping develop materials and train pastors for "The 50 Day Spiritual Adventure." I had just completed a project on worship with the Christian singer Twila Paris.

"Doug, I have something for you to pray about," David began. Well, that got my attention!

David continued, "You know how I usually write the theme book for *The 50 Day Spiritual Adventure*? Well, I have been swamped and just can't get started. So, I would like you to pray about writing this for us."

His request stunned me. I'd been writing articles for Christian magazines for nearly fifteen years and wanted *desperately* to publish a book. And now it was dropping in my lap??

"David," I said, "I don't have to pray about it! This is an answer to years of prayer!"

"Well, Doug, I think you'll want to pray about this: the manuscript must be completed in eight weeks!"

That was a challenge indeed, but I could already feel the Spirit's stirring.

"Now, we'll go over the details more in a few days," continued David, "but we'll be sending you a book contract from Victor Books/ Scripture Press. We will pay you an advance of $10,000 for this project. Will that work for you?"

Will that work for me?? Are you *kidding?*

"David, do you have time for me to tell you about why this is an answer to prayer in more ways than one?"

Since that time, I have taught (and reminded myself continually), "Where God guides, God provides."

Face Failure Without Self-Condemnation

A third aspect of a sailing mentality is seen in how we handle mistakes.

Mistakes are human. Expect problems. Frustrations and obstacles are part and parcel of the human experience. Some are of our own making and others are beyond our control. Regardless of the cause, keep your eyes on the far horizon and sail onward.

In his book, *Testament of Devotion*, Thomas Kelly frequently provides wise guidance for those likely to feel overwhelmed by failure:

> Lapses and forgettings are so frequent. Our surroundings grow so exciting. Our occupations are so exacting. But when you catch yourself again, lose no time in self-recriminations, but breathe a silent prayer for forgiveness and begin again, just where you are. Offer this broken worship up to Him and say: "This is what I am except Thou aid me." Admit no discouragement but ever return quietly to Him and wait in His Presence.
>
> …Don't grit your teeth and clench your fists and say, "I will! I will!" Relax. Take hands off. Submit yourself to God. Learn to live in the passive voice—a hard saying for Americans—and let life be willed through you. For "I will" spells not obedience.[99]

In Christ, failure is not fatal. God's grace covers our sins and our failings. That's no excuse for careless sin or what the Bible calls "high-handed" or presumptuous misdeeds (Numbers 15:30). But we know that when we get off course or even fail to steer the course God has set before us, the Lord *will* respond when we cry out.

38
Spiritual Disciplines Keep Your Inner Game of Destiny Alive

Specific spiritual exercises strengthen and focus your soul for spiritual vitality. These disciplines help keep you shipshape. They set your spiritual compass, trim your sails, and help you catch the wind of the Holy Spirit.

While I can make a case for the usefulness of all spiritual disciplines for every aspect of leadership, some are especially fitting for our Destiny, our motivation, our Why.

The three primary "pathways to spiritual vitality" that cultivate our sense of destiny are:

God's perspective renews our minds.

God's pace redeems our time.

God's presence fills our hearts.

Several specific disciplines within each of these pathways are especially helpful.

Destiny Navigates by the Eternal Perspective

God's perspective renews your mind. The spiritual disciplines of perspective help you keep your eyes on the Big Picture.

Our thoughts and perspective constantly get pulled earthward by the gravity of life. Even as rockets require massive energy to break earth's gravitational pull, so our minds require the holy energy of God's Word to break the bonds of worldly thinking.

Bible study, which I also call cognitive meditation, renews our minds. We learn to discern what Randy Frazee calls the Upper Story and the Lower Story.[100] The Lower Story is the account of everyday human experience. The Bible helps us understand both human destiny and the reality of human despair and darkness. But Scripture also provides "the story behind the lower story" that shows us the way to Life. "The Upper Story" reveals the meaning of life from the eternal perspective. We will see that there is one grand drama with many, many subplots, all serving the main action of God's will and purpose.

Wise leaders take time not merely to read the Bible but to develop a biblical understanding of life, values, and God's design for relationships. Leaders "renew their minds" (Romans 12:2) by absorbing God's wisdom and seeking to apply it in every aspect of life. Study the lives of God's great (and very human) leaders such as Abraham, Moses, Joshua, Gideon, Deborah, David, Hezekiah, Esther, Jesus, and Paul. Consider the wisdom taught in the Book of Proverbs. Let the Psalms teach you to come to the Lord in the full experience of life—in its joys and the sorrows, its victories and the defeats, its love and conflict. Make God's Word your manual for life and work.

Destiny Thrives as You Follow Jesus' Rhythm of Life

God's pace redeems your time, with time being one of the most challenging factors in a leader's life. Leaders face pressure from multiple sources and scramble to stay ahead of the avalanche.

One of my dearest friends, John, often alludes to the classic scene in *Indiana Jones and Raiders of the Lost Ark*, where Indy runs madly from the massive rolling boulder. "That's how I feel most of the time!" John says with a wince and a smile. We all know that feeling—and it's no fun!

Do we *ever* see Jesus in a hurry? Is he too busy for interruptions? He demonstrated a rhythm of engagement and withdrawal that kept him spiritually refreshed and engaged. He spent time with his disciples and followers and then withdrew for times of solitude and prayer.

We are not very kind to ourselves. We push and push and push. We work and work and work. And then we wonder why we're tired, discouraged, and joyless. We suffer from what my friend, Dave Rhodes, calls the "arrogance of unlimited capacity." We don't recognize our limits.[101]

Energy returns when you rest. Rest replenishes your spiritual, mental, and physical reserves. So, how do we learn to live at a godly pace? Consider a few suggestions.

1.   TAKE YOUR DAY OFF

I can already hear your excuses! We all have a variety of reasons (justifications) that conspire to drive us to overwork. But spiritual vitality demands that we pay attention to—and deal with—these factors. Deadlines are well-named! DEADline. Hmm... is there a bit of overexaggeration here? I'm all for the timely completion of assignments, but not for the implied consequence of failing to meet them!

A day off is a gracious provision in many cultures that allows time for catching up on personal projects, errands, and chores that can't be easily fit into one's work schedule. It's also a time for enjoying family and friends. You can learn to manage yourself, so you work diligently when you are scheduled to work, and so you can play guilt-free when you get a day off.

Don't fall for the "noble temptation" of not taking a day off! Neither the admiration from others, nor the effort to impress others with your huge responsibilities, are worth the price you'll eventually pay in loss of physical, mental, spiritual and relational well-being.

2.   ENJOY SABBATH REST[102]

A second discipline for letting God's pace redeem your time is taking your weekly Sabbath. I teach a course on spirituality for seminary students preparing for pastoral ministry. I inform them that congregations readily allow their pastors to break one of the Ten Commandments with impunity. In fact, many of their parishioners will reward them and applaud them for breaking it. What commandment? Keeping the Sabbath.

Let's be candid: workaholism is, perhaps not-so-blatantly, considered a virtue. What a sad state of affairs when pastors and congregations conspire to ignore this commandment! Since we've decided the Sabbath is optional, we're down to Nine Commandments.

And we're paying the price.

It's often pointed out that God did not give Moses the Ten Suggestions, but that's how we often treat them, especially the Sabbath.

Sabbath is *entirely* different from a day off. Sabbath is a time to honor the Lord and tend to our spiritual well-being. Few books on the Sabbath are more profound than Abraham Joshua Heschel's book *The Sabbath: Its Meaning for Modern Man*.[103] Heschel writes:

Six days we wrestle with the world, wringing profit from the earth; on the Sabbath we especially care for the need of eternity planted in the soul. The world has our hands, but our soul belongs to Someone Else.[104]

He also wrote:

Six days we live under the tyranny of things of space; on the Sabbath we try to become attuned to holiness in time, a day on which we are called…to turn from the results to the mystery of creation; from the world of creation to the creation of the world.[105]

Heschel reminds us that we are not beasts of burden who rest so we can work harder. Rest reminds us that we are meant for more than this world.

Many books give great guidance for enjoying Sabbath rest. The primary goal is taking time to connect with God, connect with your soul, and connect with the special people God has put in your life.[106]

Discover and Thrive on God's Presence Throughout the Day

You also can nurture your spiritual vitality with disciplines that help you experience God's presence filling your heart.

Too many of us limit our sense of God's presence to a few inspiring events or special moments. We just don't expect to experience God's presence daily. But we can! In fact, my experience with three brothers in Christ, all executives in midtown New York City, led me to develop a discipline I call "Preview." Hundreds of individuals have practiced and affirmed it, even calling it one of the most practical exercises they have ever used to experience God's presence throughout the day.[107]

Preview brings together prayer, holy imagination, and your calendar at the beginning of your day so that you develop an awareness of the Lord *throughout* the day.[108]

The basic plan is to schedule ten to fifteen minutes at the start of the day with your Bible, journal, and calendar. After reading your Bible and saying your normal prayers, take out your calendar (electronic or paper, it makes no difference) and then pray sequentially through your projects and appointments/responsibilities for the day.

As you pray over each event, person, and project, take a moment to listen for a nudge from the Lord. Perhaps a scripture comes to mind, or an idea. Note these in your calendar, in your journal, or in electronic notes. Then put a mark alongside each item. When I use the calendar on my phone or laptop, I add a + (plus sign) to signify a cross.

Conclude by inviting the Lord to walk with you through your day. Picture the Lord as physically present with you in conversations, meetings, and activities.

If you begin your day by previewing situations to become aware of God's presence throughout the day, it makes sense to "close the loop" and consider how the day went. You asked the Lord to guide you; so, what happened? How did God show up?[109]

The discipline of Review is another name for the Prayer of Examen. You review your day with an eye toward two dimensions:

your consciousness of God's presence as well as your conscience, especially your awareness of your own specific confessions.

In my experience, we discern God's presence more often in the memory than in the moment. When you look back over your day or week, you discern how God orchestrated events. You understand delays as times for preparation. You see "chance" connections as providential meetings that open new doors. What others call a coincidence you can call a God-incident.

When you look back, you also recognize your sins of omission as well as commission. As the Anglican prayerbook says, "We have left undone those things which we ought to have done; and we have done those things which we ought not to have done; and there is no health in us."[110]

Undertake this review in the spirit of grace, following the counsel of 1 John 1:7-9 (ESV):

> But if we walk in the light, as he is in the light, we have fellowship with one another, and the blood of Jesus his Son cleanses us from all sin. If we say we have no sin, we deceive ourselves, and the truth is not in us. If we confess our sins, he is faithful and just to forgive us our sins and to cleanse us from all unrighteousness.

It's like taking an evening shower to wash away the grit of the day. Physically, we feel thankful for the refreshment and cleansing a shower brings. Spiritually, we welcome the shower of grace that God pours on us through the Living Water of Jesus Christ. And as always, conviction is for invitation, not condemnation.

Choose One Discipline to Cultivate Your Ultimate Why

Having reviewed these disciplines, which one would be most helpful for you over the next two to three months? You might start by assessing one area that concerns you the most.

- Do you desire to make sense of your work in terms of God's coming Kingdom? Then choose a discipline for developing God's perspective, such as Bible study.
- Is it your pace of life? Then focus on Sabbath rest.
- Do you desire to become more sensitive and aware of God's presence in all circumstances? Then focus on the twin practices of Preview and Review.

"Why not try to do them all?" someone asks. The quick answer is that simplicity encourages victory. You don't want these to become burdensome. The disciplines are practices that set you free. You'll find that effective practice of *one* discipline will naturally expand your practice of others.

Don't Neglect the Broader Dimensions of Your Call

It's possible that you may fulfill your most important destiny on the way to your desired destiny—but that's not ideal![111]

Remember Mr. Holland,[112] the frustrated composer who chose to be a school music teacher to "put bread on the table?" Only at his retirement celebration did he realize that he had been composing music in the lives of his students. He was bringing music to life in their lives.

Such a living symphony will have an impact *far* beyond what any musical composition could accomplish. But because Mr. Holland had failed to understand the broader dimensions of his call, he lived for years in a state of frustration and discontent.

We turn to that broader discussion now. In addition to knowing who we are in Christ (our Identity) and how everything we do ultimately furthers God's coming Kingdom (our Destiny), we also need to grasp the mindset of Partnership with God and others.

Part Four

Partnership: Link with God's Kingdom Agenda

Jesus ... rose from supper. He laid aside his outer garments, and taking a towel, tied it around his waist. Then he poured water into a basin and began to wash the disciples' feet and to wipe them with the towel that was wrapped around him.

—JOHN 13:3, 4-5

Leaders cultivate a mindset of partnership as they express their identity and pursue their destiny. A.W. Tozer clearly stated this vision:

"Let [people] sanctify the Lord God in their hearts and they can thereafter do no common act. All they do is good and acceptable to God through Jesus Christ. For such people, living itself will be sacramental and the whole world a sanctuary."[113]

Such leaders become increasingly aware that they must actively seek to fulfill Jesus' petition, "Thy Kingdom come, Thy will be done on earth as it is in heaven." They recognize they are partners in God's continuing work in this world. This means that the things they do, whatever those things are, will always be done *differently*.

Whatever you do, work at it with all your heart, as working for the Lord, not for human masters, since you know that you will receive an inheritance from the Lord as a reward. It is the Lord Christ you are serving.

—PAUL IN COLOSSIANS 3:23-24 (NIV)

The love of our neighbor is the only door out of the dungeon of self.

—GEORGE MACDONALD[114]

With a good conscience our only sure reward, with history the final judge of our deeds, let us go forth to lead the land we love, asking his blessing and his help, but knowing that here on earth, God's work must truly be our own.

—JOHN F. KENNEDY'S 1961 INAUGURAL ADDRESS, CONCLUDING SENTENCE

Your work in the world is as sacred as the work of a pastor in a church. It is not what you do that determines whether your work is sacred or secular; it is why you do it. The motive is everything. Sanctify the Lord God in your heart and nothing you do is simply a common act. Everything is acceptable to God through Jesus Christ. When you live and work this way, living itself will be sacramental and the whole world a sanctuary.

—A.W. TOZER (PARAPHRASED)[115]

Enemy-occupied territory— that is what this world is. Christianity is the story of how the rightful king has landed, you might say landed in disguise and is calling us all to take part in a great campaign of sabotage.

—C. S. LEWIS[116]

39
Do Everything Differently

The August 28, 2007 edition of the *Wall Street Journal* published a story about commercial airline pilot Captain Denny Flanagan, who certainly did his job differently.

Capt. Denny Flanagan is a rare bird in today's frustration-filled air-travel world—a pilot who goes out of his way to make flying fun for passengers.

When pets travel in cargo compartments, the [veteran] pilot snaps pictures of them with his cell phone camera, then shows owners that their animals are on board. In the air he has flight attendants raffle off ten percent discount coupons. He writes notes to first-class passengers and…frequent fliers on the back of his business card, addressing them by name and thanking them for their business. If flights are delayed or diverted to other cities because of storms, Capt. Flanagan tries to find a McDonald's where he can order 200 hamburgers, or a snack shop that has apples or bananas he can hand out… When unaccompanied children are on his flights, he personally calls parents with reassuring updates. "I picked up the phone and he said, 'This is the captain from your son's flight,'" said Kenneth Klein, whose 12-year-old son was delayed by thunderstorms in Chicago last month on a trip from Los Angeles to see his grandfather in Toronto. "It was unbelievable. One of the big problems is kids sit on planes, and no one tells you what's happening, and this was the exact opposite." Capt. Flanagan is so unusual there's a blog about him on FlyerTalk.com. One hardened road warrior wrote, "For the life of me, I can't figure out what this guy's ulterior motive is…"[117]

I first heard this story from the Rev. Dr. Vic Pentz, then Senior Pastor of Peachtree Presbyterian Church in Atlanta. Vic echoed my sentiments when he said, "I don't know Captain Flanagan, but I'd love to think his motive is serving God."

Although we don't know Captain Flanagan's motives, we can certainly draw from his model. Especially if we embrace God's call in Colossians 3:23 (NIV):

> Whatever you do, work at it with all your heart, as working for the Lord, not for human masters, since you know that you will receive an inheritance from the Lord as a reward. It is the Lord Christ you are serving.

A common misconception declares that "being a full-time Christian" means being a pastor, a minister, or someone in full-time ministry. Nothing could be further from the truth. A full-time disciple is essentially someone who serves the Lord in the way they do everything they do. That's what I mean when I say, "We won't necessarily do different things, but we'll do everything differently."

You may still lead a sales team, but you do so with respect and integrity. You may still be a graphic designer, but you approach your work and your clients with a prayerful attitude, always giving your best. You listen for the Lord and "keep your sail in the wind," expecting the Lord's leading. It's how we do anything we do that makes the difference.

40

Leaders Are God's Partners in Kingdom Work

The souls of leaders are rooted in identity and fixed on destiny; everything in between is partnership and stewardship.

From the account of creation in Genesis throughout the entire Old and New Testaments, God creates, calls, and charges people to partner with God in the care and governance of this world. Work is *not* part of the curse. Work was part of God's original purpose for humanity:

> Then God said, "Let us make mankind in our image, in our likeness, so that they may rule over the fish in the sea and the birds in the sky, over the livestock and all the wild animals, and over all the creatures that move along the ground … ."
>
> The Lord God took the man and put him in the Garden of Eden to work it and take care of it. (Genesis 1:26; 2:15, ESV).

God created humans to care for and develop God's creation. As someone has said, "God created us to win from creation its hospitality." The curse was the consequence of humanity's disobedience. Ever since, as humanity resisted God, so has creation resisted humanity.

Everything changes when we understand that everything we do, we do as God's partners. Colossians 3:23-24 describes a disciple's mindset. Disciples do not compartmentalize life. Partnership means we *always* seek God's coming kingdom in everything we do.

The kingdom of God was a central concept in Jesus' teaching and mission. C. H. Dodd writes, "The 'Kingdom of God' is…the manifestation and effective assertion of the divine sovereignty against all the evils of the world."[118] Let's take a few moments to explore and understand God's strategy.

As mentioned earlier, God consistently involves humanity as partners in his ongoing work. This principle, "God makes, we shape," communicates God's methodology for bringing the kingdom of God "on earth as it is in heaven."

Jesus won a decisive victory through his incarnation, life, death, resurrection, and ascension. We cannot add anything to that. But God has chosen to involve us in the implementation and application of Jesus' accomplishments around the globe, across the ages, and for every age and stage of life. One day, the time finally will come when we will hear "loud voices in heaven, saying, 'The kingdom of the world has become the kingdom of our Lord and of his Christ, and he shall reign forever and ever'" (Revelation 11:15, ESV). Until that day, however, we have holy work to do.

This concept—that a gap of time exists between Jesus' securing victory and all of creation enjoying the completeness of that victory—has many analogies in history. German theologian Oscar Cullmann offered one example that helps us understand how Satan and the forces of evil, though defeated, still have great influence in this world. Cullman reminds us that most military experts agree that victory for the Allies in World War II was assured on D-Day (June 6, 1944), the day Allied forces successfully invaded Nazi-occupied Europe on the beaches of Normandy, France. When Germany failed to prevent the invasion, victory for the British, American, and Canadian forces was inevitable. But it took eleven months for the Allies to end the war. During this time, thousands of men lost their lives in the bloodiest battles of the entire conflict. Cullman points out that the arrival of victory (V-E Day May 8, 1945) was assured by the invasion on D-Day but not realized without the subsequent battles.

We are in a similar position as Christians: the final and full establishment of the kingdom of God, with Christ as its head, was assured at the resurrection; but we have yet to realize its fullness. That day is coming, but it is not yet.[119]

So, we speak of "the already and the not yet."

Yes, Jesus has *already* won the ultimate victory, but that victory is *not yet* completely realized in everyday life. We are engaged in the continuing conflict. While some resist the analogy, Paul reminds us that we are soldiers involved in spiritual warfare. That's why he exhorted Timothy, "Endure hardship with us like a good soldier of Christ Jesus" (2 Timothy 2:3, NLT). "We must equip ourselves by allowing the power of the Spirit to come into our lives and work through us to defeat the enemy."[120]

Later in this section we'll see how Daniel, exiled in Babylon, provides a powerful illustration of a person who excelled in his public work without compromising his devotion to God. We'll also see how his fellow exiles also were called to be channels of God's grace in a foreign land. Our location doesn't contradict our calling.

What Is a "Partner"?

The word "partner" highlights the dual dynamic of dependence and interdependence. Partners communicate. They work together. They honor an agreement (covenant) together. While no one would claim that God "needs" us as partners, Scripture is clear that God has chosen to rely on us.

Jesus confirms our partnership when he promises we would bear fruit and do even greater works than he accomplished:

"Truly, truly, I say to you, whoever believes in me will also do the works that I do; and greater works than these will he do, because I am going to the Father. Whatever you ask in my name, this I will do, that the Father may be glorified in the Son. If you ask me anything in my name, I will do it" (John 14:12-14, ESV).

He also said:

"You did not choose me, but I chose you and appointed you that you should go and bear fruit and that your fruit should abide, so that whatever you ask the Father in my name, he may give it to you" (John 15:16, ESV).

God speaks of his people as his highly functioning body in this world:

"For just as the body is one and has many members, and all the members of the body, though many, are one body, so it is with Christ. For in one Spirit we were all baptized into one body— Jews or Greeks, slaves or free—and all were made to drink of one Spirit" (1 Corinthians 12:12-13, ESV).

God created us to do good works, the fruit of faith in Christ:

"For by grace you have been saved through faith. And this is not your own doing; it is the gift of God, not a result of works, so that no one may boast. For we are his workmanship, created in Christ Jesus for good works, which God prepared before-hand, that we should walk in them" (Ephesians 2:8-10, ESV).

As disciples and as leaders, we articulate our purpose in this way: "I am your partner, Lord, in this place, at this time, with these people, and these tasks."

Partnership shapes our definition of success. Here's are some of my working definitions of success: "Pursuing and achieving God's purposes as I steward the life entrusted to me for God's glory and my joy." Another version of success for me sounds like this: "Keeping my First Love first, I seek to accomplish as much as possible for God's coming kingdom, working God's way in God's power through the gifts and opportunities God provides."

How do you define success? I encourage you to write several definitions, then live with them for a while. Refine them and see which one feels like it best communicates your heart and mind.

And remember: We can do *everything* differently when we live and lead from the soul.

41
Ministry in the Marketplace

Some people have the idea that ministry happens at church, or at least only through those officially ordained as pastors or ministers. As I've already said, nothing could be further from the truth.

God's people (often called the laity, or lay people, based on the Greek term *laos*, which means "people") are scattered across the spectrum of society and business. They have credibility, access, and applicable know-how with others that those in "official" ordained ministry often lack.

People outside the church tend to be suspicious of pastors. In fact, when people who don't know me ask what I do, I always begin by saying, "I'm a consultant." When they ask follow-up questions, I usually have a bit of fun, saying things like, "I am involved in long—*really long*—range planning. I work for a large multi-national organization that has been around for years, even centuries. You could also say that I'm a type of life coach, and a teacher…"[121] By this point, my new "friend" is quite puzzled and curious to have a specific title or label. When I finally say, "I'm a pastor," they usually laugh and say they didn't see that coming.

Still, the fact remains that "everyday" Christians, especially leaders who have demonstrated effectiveness, have far more appeal and interest to the world than "religious professionals" (I do *not* like that designation!). We all need to recognize this reality and make the most of it.

While pastoring the First Presbyterian Church of Hollywood, Richard Halverson (later sixtieth chaplain of the United States Senate) learned what he called a "significant" lesson when he was approached by a leading layman who had been elected president of the local school board. This meant a key layman would have to drop some of his church responsibilities. At first, Pastor Halverson resented the thought of losing so active a worker. After more consideration, however, he reached a very different conclusion. In *How I Changed My Thinking About the Church*, he wrote:

As I pondered the loss of this fine young man…I asked…"How many do we need to really do the work of the organization of this church?"…many of the men and women in the church had several jobs…They were very busy with the ecclesiastical establishment. But suppose that each could hold only one job, how many people would it take to do the work of that large congregation? At the time, the membership was about 7,000. To my amazement, I found that it would require only 365 to do the work that was required to maintain the program of the First Presbyterian Church of Hollywood…. This meant that most of the members of the church could never have a job in the institution. It followed…that if the work of the church is what is done for the institution, very few, relatively speaking, will ever have an opportunity to do the work of the church.[122]

Marketplace or workplace ministry is not second-class ministry. It lies at the heart of God's strategy to change the world. It's the strategy of salt that seasons, of light that pierces the darkness.

It's the strategy of infiltration.

42
Daniel: God's Servant in a Pagan Government

I'm not sure I like the term "pagan government," but you get the idea. The Old Testament story of Daniel tells us about the courage and effective leadership of a Jewish youth who rose to the top of the Babylonian government without compromising his identity or his standards of conduct.

The fulfillment of God's long-threatened judgment on the Israelites through the Babylonian King Nebuchadnezzar devastated the Hebrew nation. His troops tore down the walls of Jerusalem and razed Solomon's temple. We read the account in 2 Chronicles 36:19-20 (ESV):

> And they burned the house of God and broke down the wall of Jerusalem and burned all its palaces with fire and destroyed all its precious vessels. He took into exile in Babylon those who had escaped from the sword, and they became servants to him and to his sons until the establishment of the kingdom of Persia [the empire that in seventy years would destroy Babylon].

The Babylonians deported the defeated Jews in three separate incidents. The first came in 605 BC, when Nebuchadnezzar first defeated Israel; Daniel and friends were among this first wave (see 2 Kings 20:14). A second major wave occurred in 597 BC, when Ezekiel and other leaders went into exile (see 2 Kings 24:11-16). The third wave happened with the nation's final defeat in 586 BC, preceded by the destruction of Jerusalem (see 2 Kings 25:1-21).

From the Book of Daniel, we learn that Daniel ended up in the very heart of the Babylonian empire, in the palace of the king himself—Judah's archenemy! The exiles who had arrived with Daniel were the cream of Jerusalem's society and culture. Daniel and three of his friends were tapped immediately for their leadership potential and brought into the King's palace to become part of what we might call "Nebuchadnezzar's Leadership Academy."

Can you imagine the pressure Daniel and his friends must have felt? But the situation did not intimidate them. Why not? Because they had established their identity from the very outset of their captivity.

Scripture tells us, "But Daniel resolved that he would not defile himself with the king's food, or with the wine that he drank. Therefore, he asked the chief of the eunuchs to allow him not to defile himself" (Daniel 1:8, ESV). The servant granted this request to eat "kosher" (as we would now say). The results were impressive:

> At the end of ten days it was seen that they were better in appearance and fatter in flesh than all the youths who ate the king's food. So the steward took away their food and the wine they were to drink and gave them vegetables (Daniel 1:15-16, ESV).

These results grew even more impressive when Nebuchadnezzar himself tested their training:

> As for these four youths, God gave them learning and skill in all literature and wisdom, and Daniel had understanding in all visions and dreams. At the end of the time, when the king had commanded that they should be brought in, the chief of the eunuchs brought them in before Nebuchadnezzar. And the king spoke with them, and among all of them none was found like Daniel, Hananiah, Mishael, and Azariah. Therefore they stood before the king. And in every matter of wisdom and understanding about which the king inquired of them, he found them ten times better than all the magicians and enchanters that were in all his kingdom. And Daniel was there until the first year of King Cyrus (Daniel 1:17-21, ESV).

Daniel played a key leadership role in the Babylonian government for approximately seventy years![123] During that time, the loyalty of Daniel and his Jewish colleagues to God was frequently tested in dramatic ways (see Daniel 3 and Daniel 6). But they never wavered in their faithfulness.

Daniel's witness seems to have been more behavioral than verbal. He prayed three times a day in front of his open apartment window where others could see him. He did not deliberately antagonize his opponents, but neither did he alter his behavior to avoid consequences.

We cannot change everything, but we can influence those areas where we have control. Don't compartmentalize your faith! You can let your light shine in the coffee shop, the classroom, or the office.

Too often we hide our light out of fear, ignorance, distraction, or by following our own ungodly habits and desires. It's time to repent, if necessary, and accept our call to be God's change-agents in this world.

43
Holy Saboteurs

Like Daniel, Jesus' followers live in enemy-occupied territory. God our King has landed in disguise and is calling us to take part in a great campaign of sabotage. Since God's kingdom is a very different world, we need to learn (as Daniel illustrates) how to seek God's kingdom first in the middle of the common activities and ventures of life.

The term "holy saboteurs" comes from C. S. Lewis:

> One of the things that surprised me when I first read the New Testament seriously was that it talked so much about a Dark Power in the universe–a mighty evil spirit who was held to be the Power behind death and disease, and sin. The difference is that Christianity thinks this Dark Power was created by God, and was good when he was created, and went wrong. Christianity agrees with Dualism that this universe is at war. But it does not think this is a war between independent powers. It thinks it is a civil war, a rebellion, and that we are living in a part of the universe occupied by the rebel. Enemy-occupied territory– that is what this world is.

> Christianity is the story of how the rightful king has landed, you might say landed in disguise and is calling us all to take part in a great campaign of sabotage. When you go to church you are really listening-in to the secret wireless from our friends: that is why the enemy is so anxious to prevent us from going."[124]

God's people are scattered throughout the world and at every level of society. Leaders, especially, can exercise dramatic influence for the ethical and redemptive working of business. Gibbs and Morton declare:

> Laity are the frontline troops of God's army; these are the men and women who have to keep the faith and survive in the gray world of business negotiations, labor union loyalties, local government contracts, party caucuses, popular journalism,

competitive television and the like. Their nurture and support should be the first concern of the church.[125]

Jesus' followers are in this world as "holy saboteurs," seeking to bring God's truth, power, and influence into all aspects of life. A saboteur looks for places of weakness or vulnerability and exploits them for their purposes. Jesus' followers seek to defeat the powers of darkness by bringing God's light and love into the places of weakness, heartache, vulnerability and brokenness.

Holy Saboteurs tear down the walls that keep people apart so that they can be reconciled in Christ.

Holy Saboteurs expose lies by proclaiming the truth that sets people free.

Holy Saboteurs shatter complacency so that people engage intentionally in the abundant and eternal life of God in Christ.

Holy Saboteurs afflict the comfortable so that they may awaken from the numbness of false security.

Holy Saboteurs come alongside the doubters, urging them to use those doubts as doorways to deeper faith and understanding.

Leader, be a Holy Saboteur! Bring God's light and love into dark places of weakness, heartache, vulnerability and brokenness.

44

We're Not Just Passing Through

An old saying complains that Christians can be so heavenly-minded that they're no earthly good. But that's just the opposite of what we're supposed to be. God calls his people to make a difference wherever they are. That was the message the prophet Jeremiah gave to the Jews living in exile in Babylon. We've mentioned Jeremiah 29:4[126], but let's go a bit deeper.

The exiles living in Babylon were the cream of society and culture from Jerusalem. They all had a question: "How long will we remain in exile? Is this just a brief punishment to get our attention? Or is God planning something longer?"

A false prophet named Hananiah had been spreading a bogus teaching that the exiles would return to Jerusalem in just two years (see Jeremiah 26). But God's true prophet, Jeremiah, had announced that they would remain in Babylon for seven decades.[127] Jeremiah rebuked Hananiah and then prophesied that this false prophet would die that very year. And in fact, Hananiah died several months after delivering his false prophecy (see Jeremiah 26:16)!

So, what should God's people do when once they realized they would not be returning to their homeland for a very long time? Read again what God's told the people through Jeremiah:

Thus says the LORD of hosts, the God of Israel, to all the exiles whom I have sent into exile from Jerusalem to Babylon: Build houses and live in them; plant gardens and eat their produce. Take wives and have sons and daughters; take wives for your sons, and give your daughters in marriage, that they may bear sons and daughters; multiply there, and do not decrease. But seek the welfare of the city where I have sent you into exile, and pray to the Lord on its behalf, for in its welfare you will find your welfare" (Jeremiah 29:4-7, ESV).

Witness to God's Purpose in All Activities of Life

Jeremiah exhorted the exiles to accept that they would remain in Babylon for a long time. The moment had come to unpack their suitcases and unload the boxes as concrete expressions of settling down and putting down roots (see Jeremiah 29:5, 6).

They were to build—in contrast to destruction they had seen.

They were to plant—to settle down and make a living off the land, not simply "get by" for the time being. It takes long periods of time for crops to mature and bear fruit. So, invest in the ground, make a productive place for yourself.

Eat with contentment, even if some of the foods differ from what you're used to.

Marry and have families. Don't postpone. Don't be afraid of having children in a "foreign culture." Learn how to be God's people in the middle of alien society.

The Israelites needed to learn that God's presence and power were not restricted to "the Holy Land." A primary assumption of ancient cultures was that their "gods" had power only in a specific locale. The exiles learned that YHWH (Exodus 3:14) was present and active *everywhere*.

We, too, are called to participate in the ventures of common life with a clear and consistent focus on the Lord "in whom we live and move and have our being" (Acts 17:28, ESV).

Build. Work. Raise our families in a godly way in the middle of an often-godless culture. God has a purpose for us to "settle down and settle in." It's not simply for our own sakes, but so that you will...

Work for God's Blessing Wherever You Live

The exiles had a second charge, to "seek the peace (well-being) of the city and community" (see Jeremiah 29:7-14). They were to seek this peace and prosperity for the benefit of all, not as some "health and wealth gospel," but as loving stewardship and responsible engagement.

Your call to be salt and light means you work to make the culture at least conducive to Christian living. We are not called, nor are we able, to create a theocracy in which the culture completely represents Christian values.[128] We are wise, however, to do everything reasonable to create the maximum space and opportunity for believers to live out their faith, believing that this will benefit *all* people. In part, this is what Paul intended when he wrote:

First of all, then, I urge that supplications, prayers, intercessions, and thanksgivings be made for all people, for kings and all who are in high positions, *that we may lead a peaceful and quiet life, godly and dignified in every way.* This is good, and it is pleasing in the sight of God our Savior, who desires all people to be saved and to come to the knowledge of the truth (1 Timothy 2:1-4, ESV, emphasis added).

The word "welfare" in Jeremiah 29:7 is a translation of the Hebrew term *shalom.* We are to work for the peace—*shalom*—of the city. *Shalom* encompasses a wide range of positive, beneficial circumstances: health, prosperity, peace, wholeness, completeness, well-being, the absence of strife. This kind of *shalom* is based on peace with God: that is, being in a right relationship with God through grace and the fruit of obedience.

What does peace look like in our communities? Peace comes when we find creative ways to show our community that we care. In his sermon on this topic, Pastor Vic Pentz[129] described his congregation's response when Atlanta police officer, Mark Cross, a member of Peachtree Presbyterian Church in Atlanta, died in the line of duty. The congregation's leadership prayed about how to honor him. They came to the congregation with a proposal to honor Mark by purchasing life insurance policies for all 1,700 police officers of Atlanta.

As you might imagine, they stunned the city!

Make a Difference with Your Gifts and Involvement

Let's consider another example emerging from the Reformers' strategy of transforming the arts and culture to reflect God's *shalom.* Johann Sebastian Bach, the master of Baroque music, signed all his works with the phrase *Soli Deo Gloria,* meaning "to God alone be the glory."

Today, Jesus has many followers in Hollywood. The mission statement of one organization called Act One describes it as "a Christian community of entertainment industry professionals who train and equip storytellers to create works of truth, goodness and beauty."[130] Act One offers a variety of programs, including Writing for Film & Television and The Producing & Entertainment Executive. Members of the faculty work for all the major movie and television studios and have produced top-rated movies and programs.

Partner with God through Intercession and Prayer

Whenever I preached on these themes, I regularly focused on various vocations, giving them special attention and prayer. Following one service where we focused on teachers, I received the following email:

Hi Pastor Doug,

I have been especially stressed at work. Public school teachers are constantly under attack and expected to work miracles with little support. But I digress. Back to my point, while voicing my work frustrations with my daughter's teacher (who was a public school teacher for 20 years and now teaches at a Christian school), she shared that she and some fellow teachers met every morning before school for fellowship and prayer. As I drove to school, several things came to mind:

1) I remember last Sunday you mentioned how a teacher prayed for her students every day and that it changed her (something I really needed to hear).

2) I thought about a conversation I had with a friend who teaches in my district, and she expressed her lack of enthusiasm and joy at work and said that other teachers at her school felt the same way. Morale is very low in my district.

3) Could we really pray and ask for God's help in a public school? What my daughter's teacher said really resonated with me. When I got to school, I saw another teacher who I knew was a Christian and proposed the idea to her. She was excited and said she would talk to other teachers who might be interested, and I would speak to our principal about any "rules" we needed to follow.

The result is that on Monday morning, 7 or 8 of us are going to meet in a teacher's room before school to pray for our school and our students. I would never have taken this step if not for your series, Pastor. I thank you for helping me "push the limits" of my faith. I don't always listen to God, and don't always like what He tells me, but I have to remember that He knows better than I do. I can't wait to see how God works in my and the other teachers' lives at school. And who says that God has no place in public education…!

Thanks for letting me share. See you Sunday![131]

As Jesus' followers, we partner with God to seek the peace (*shalom*) and well-being of our communities, our schools, our businesses, our neighborhoods. We engage in the life of our communities, being salt and light for the world to "taste (salt) and see (light) that the LORD is good!" (Psalm 34:8, with my additions). We are partners with God to bring God's shalom into every dimension of our communities. That is perhaps your primary job as a leader.

45
Our Everyday Life Mindset

Partnership is the basis for our mindset in life.

Identity defines our *meaning* in life. We can answer questions concerning where we came from and who we are as beings created by God. Our identity assures us of our value as members of God's family. We know who we are and whose we are. We know our place in the universe.

Destiny establishes our *motivation* for life. We know God has put us on Earth for His purposes and that we live with The End—our eternal destiny—in mind. This is our "Why," our direction and energy in life.

Partnership frames our *mindset* for living out our God-given identity. This is our "How" and "When" for life, shaping our approach and methods for all we think, say, and do, wherever we live, work, serve, or play.

Presbyterian pastor, Richard Halverson, frequently gave the following benediction[132] at the conclusion of his church's worship services:

> You go nowhere by accident.
> Wherever you go, God is sending you;
> wherever you are, God has put you there.
> God has a purpose in your being there.
> Christ who indwells you has something He wants to do through
> you where you are.
> Believe this and go in his grace and love and power.

I recommend that you restate this benediction in personal terms appropriate to yourself:

> I go nowhere by accident.
> Wherever I go, God is sending me;
> wherever I am, God has put me there.
> God has a purpose in my being there.
> Christ who indwells me has something He wants to do through

me where I am.
I believe this and go in His grace and love and power.

These words give us a mindset that changes our approach to everything. It transforms every moment and every interaction. We live with anticipation because we see ourselves as active partners in God's work. God is actively, personally, immediately involved in our lives. Such an attitude generates energy and makes us alert to opportunities and possibilities we would otherwise overlook or ignore.

What insights have you gained thus far through *Shaping A Leader's Soul*? Ponder them deeply—and then consider the process of living out your identity in the marketplace.

46
Embrace Your Biblical Identity in the Workplace

It's pretty straight forward: Be the person God created you to be wherever you are. Don't change faces, value systems, priorities, or language depending on whether you're at work or at a Bible study, whether you're traveling or at home. Be consistent.

I'll always remember the time I was introduced to someone with whom I shared many mutual acquaintances. When I mentioned one man, a leader in the congregation I served, this new friend responded, "He goes to church?!?! You'd never know it!"

Wow! That's not something you ever want to hear about one of your leaders!

Only one thing is riskier than being identified as a Christ follower, and that is not being identified as one. Jesus declared, "For whoever is ashamed of me and of my words in this adulterous and sinful generation, of him will the Son of Man also be ashamed when he comes in the glory of his Father with the holy angels" (Mark 8:38, ESV).

What's the best way to make your identity known? Pray about this and trust the Holy Spirit to guide you. Listen to comments others make. If someone says, "Have a blessed day," for example, that's often a signal of faith. You can follow up with, "I like that word, 'blessed.' Thank you." Or you can make simple statements, such as, "I'll be praying for you in that situation"—and then watch how people respond.

A more deliberate move might be to offer a weekly Bible study before work or at lunch time for those interested. Be relaxed and creative. Be natural and watch God open the doors. That's a clear opportunity to pull in your oars and put up your sail to catch the moving of God's Spirit!

What Does It Look Like to Cultivate a Biblical Identity in the Workplace?

When you identify yourself as a Jesus follower, it's essential to live like one. Consider a few concrete suggestions for living out your faith at work.

Remind yourself daily that God has put you in this place, at this time, for His purposes. You are where God wants you until he communicates or reveals other plans. Continually look at your work through the lens of discipleship. Ask yourself, "How would Jesus do this? What's important to the Lord in this situation?" Have a symbol or token in your workspace that will help remind you of this.

Be ready to speak about what you believe. Although you do not have to be an aggressive evangelist,[133] God calls all of us to be his witnesses, ready to share our experience at the appropriate time. "In your hearts honor Christ the Lord as holy, always being prepared to make a defense to anyone who asks you for a reason for the hope that is in you; yet do it with gentleness and respect" (1 Peter 3:15, ESV).

Treat everyone with dignity and respect—and expect them to do likewise. Paul writes, "Rather, in humility value others above yourselves, not looking to your own interests but each of you to the interests of the others" (Philippians 2:3-4, NIV). We don't think less of ourselves, but we do think more of others. This attitude of mutual caring can be contagious, creating a powerful sense of team and teamwork.

Honor boundaries. Too often a leader takes advantage of the position to exercise freedoms not readily available to employees, such as a more flexible schedule or the advantages of an expense account. No one can question these. But employees do have a right to their non-work time. Assigning an urgent project at the last minute, one demanding that an employee change plans and even give up a weekend, can violate boundaries. In a healthy workplace, the boss explains the situation and asks team members to enter the dilemma. They can offer to help in ways that allow them to honor any commitments they've made or responsibilities they have outside of work.

Practice appropriate assertiveness. Honesty and candor ensure the health of relationships, especially in teams. When I began serving a new congregation, I stepped right into a conflict that threatened to divide the church. Things went well for the first few weeks, but then some phone calls started coming in. One group of callers said it was time I thought about re-establishing a ministry with college students (called Seekers), otherwise the church would lose the rising generation.

The other group of callers warned me not to start the Seekers ministry again, because it was one of the reasons the last pastor left and would probably split the church completely.

As a young pastor, I had not always known how to manage conflict. I often remained silent or tried to work "behind the scenes," but neither option proved very effective. Before coming to this new congregation, I had made a list of things I would do differently in ministry. The two most prominent were: "Walk in the light," and "Hold up a mirror."

One exceptionally corrosive tendency of leaders is to conspire with unhealthy group dynamics through silence and avoidance. But 1 John 1:7(NIV) says, "But if we walk in the light, as he is in the light, we have fellowship with one another, and the blood of Jesus, his Son, purifies us from all sin." Walking in the light means bringing the secrets or problems to light so everyone can consider a godly response. Like mildew, sin and unhealthiness grow in the dark but die in the light. Sunlight is the best disinfectant.

Holding up a mirror is a key means to walking in the light. If the leader, or anyone else in the group, notices unhealthy dynamics (such as anger, antagonism, sarcasm, or sabotage) in the group dynamics, they can intervene and intentionally "reflect" back to the group what they are observing or perceiving. The conversation then focuses on identifying the issue(s) that have disrupted the group and trying to do their best to resolve them before proceeding with the business.

These principles (new to me) were put to the test in my first weeks with this new congregation. I called for a special gathering of the elders. In our meeting, I began with the words from Philippians 4:6 and shared my heart with them:

> "Paul told us, 'Have no anxiety about anything…' Well, I need you to know I am very anxious. I want to bring some things to light that have been happening to me. Some of you have begun calling me and saying we need to re-start the Seekers ministry or the church will die. Others have been calling me and warning me not to start the Seekers because the church would split. I am not smart enough to know what to do, but I do know that this may be the shortest pastorate in the history of this church if we don't work through this. Where do you suggest we go from here?"

After a few moments of silence, one person self-identified as an "anti-Seekers" caller. A moment later, another person self-identified as a "pro-Seekers" caller. Both began to talk—and it was as if I wasn't even in the room. The group began to articulate various fears and concerns, hopes and dreams, in love and candor.[134] Within an hour or so, they reached a decision. They agreed to form a leadership team to develop a plan to restart the group, taking into consideration the concerns shared. Our meeting concluded with everyone kneeling in prayer.

I knew this meeting could have cost me my job—but I saw honesty as the only way to move forward … and forward we went! I continued there for more than eleven years of fruitful ministry. One of my greatest mementos from my decades of ministry is a crystal bowl the elders of that church gave me when I left. It's engraved with the words, "Walk in the Light."

47
Motives

A pastor friend asked if we could meet for lunch to discuss his interest in writing books. We began our conversation about the topics that most interested him, but then the conversation took an unexpected turn.

"What about your ego and pride?" he asked. "Aren't you concerned that you're writing for the wrong reasons?"

I did not expect that.

Sooner or later, most leaders despair over having impure or mixed motives. By pure, we think of altruistic, non-selfish, non-self-centered desires. In my own experience, I felt passionate about people coming to know Jesus Christ, to love and understand God's Word, and to serve God's purposes in the world. At the same time, I wanted to be valued, to be recognized, to have a broader influence, and to earn a comfortable income for our family.

When we recognize the mixture of "good" and "self-interest" motives, we may feel tempted to despair. For my pastor-perhaps-author friend, this was a reason *not* to write. How can we possibly escape mixed motives? Frankly, that's an easy one to answer.

We can't!

This very tension, however, can become a stimulus for soul care and a source for spiritual growth.

While the previous entire section on Destiny focused on our overall motivation in life, which is living for God's coming kingdom, in this section we'll look at our day-to-day motives.

Both Kinds of *Yetzer*

In his *Genesis* commentary comments on Noah's flood, Dennis Prager has a section titled "We need both the Good Urge and the Bad Urge." He writes:

> The Hebrew word *yetzer* ... is often translated as the creative "urge" or "impulse"... The human being, Judaism teaches, has a good *yetzer* and a bad *yetzer*, and they are in permanent

conflict. However, Judaism also has long held that we need both *yetzers*... "Were it not for evil inclination," the Midrash teaches, "men would not build homes, take wives, have children, or engage in business." In other words, we do a variety of good things for very mixed, sometimes purely selfish, motives.[135]

While this is a challenging concept for sure, it gives us reasonable pause. In fact, the apostle Paul warns us against the possibility of fully discerning our motives:

> But with me it is a very small thing that I should be judged by you or by any human court. In fact, I do not even judge myself. For I am not aware of anything against myself, but I am not thereby acquitted. It is the Lord who judges me. Therefore do not pronounce judgment before the time, before the Lord comes, who will bring to light the things now hidden in darkness and will disclose the purposes of the heart. Then each one will receive his commendation from God (1 Corinthians 4:3-5, ESV).

The message for us here is self-awareness rooted in God's gracious acceptance of our humanity and the human condition, combined with the courage to monitor and manage our choices. The executive who piles up riches "for the sake of the family" (that he or she ignores in the process) is foolish. The day of reckoning comes with many possible consequences, such as divorce, estrangement from children, and even health maladies.

As with all other aspects of our fallen humanity, we admit our sin, repent, and press on toward the goals of our redemptive, upward call in Christ.

So, you might be wondering, how did I respond to my ambivalent aspiring author friend? "I think about the value books have played in my life, no matter what the authors' motives were," I told him. "As a follower of Jesus, I want to seek God's glory above all. I also know that I am a fallen human being renewed by the Spirit. So, as with everything else I do, I give my best and leave the results to God."

My friend must have gotten over the issue because he later published his first book.

And it's quite good.

Ulterior and Ultimate Motives

Another aspect of motives seems a bit more subtle but is every bit as important. It's seen, for example, in a situation where Sarah and I are intentional about reaching out to our neighbors. We want to provide opportunities for them to experience God's love in practical ways. We hope they will be open to the gospel and to attending church.

But are we doing this so they will attend our church so that our attendance will grow? So that they give to *our* offering? Do we have an ulterior motive for our evangelism that is more concerned with our benefit than theirs?

Eric Swanson and Sam Williams, in their book *To Transform a City*, use the phrase "ulterior versus ultimate" to describe the different nuances of the common motives at work in our lives and in building relationships with others:

> Ulterior means something is intentionally kept concealed. An ulterior motive is usually manipulative. It's when we do or say one thing out in the open but intend or mean another thing in private.
>
> Ultimate means the farthest point of a journey. An ultimate goal is an eventual point or a longed-for destination. Examples are when a person begins college hoping to become a physician one day or when a kid starts playing basketball with dreams of one day playing in the NBA.[136]

If we are trying to share the gospel with our neighbors for our own benefit, that ulterior motive falls into the category of self-serving and therefore requires repentance.[137] Instead, we seek to cultivate the ultimate goal and motive of our neighbors' present and eternal well-being in everything we do. This is yet another description of Destiny: Focusing on the Ultimate Why.

48
Power Trips

I was coming alongside a congregation embroiled in significant conflict over the termination of a beloved staff member. They had a clear, documented rationale for the termination. The question, as is often the case, concerned how the change was being implemented.

The prevailing stance of the leadership was what I would call a "strong man" display of power. They felt that "people need to see that this staff person can't continue to ignore us and take advantage of us."

As I prayed during the leadership team's deliberations, the story of Rehoboam's mistake came to mind. Certain overburdened Israelites had approached Rehoboam, Solomon's son and successor, to consider softening the hard demands Solomon had made on them for all his building programs. "Your father made our yoke heavy," they said to him. "Now therefore lighten the hard service of your father and his heavy yoke on us, and we will serve you." Rehoboam replied, "Go away for three days, then come again to me." So they went away (2 Kings 12:4-5, ESV).

Rehoboam first consulted the older advisors who had counseled Solomon. They advised him to grant the people's request. "If you will be a servant to this people today and serve them and speak good words to them when you answer them, then they will be your servants forever," they said (2 Kings 12:4-5, ESV). But then Rehoboam asked his youthful advisors, who gave the opposite advice. "Thus shall you speak to this people who said to you, 'Your father made our yoke heavy, but you lighten it for us,' thus shall you say to them, 'My little finger is thicker than my father's thighs. And now, whereas my father laid on you a heavy yoke, I will add to your yoke. My father disciplined you with whips, but I will discipline you with scorpions'" (2 Kings 12:10-11, ESV). Rehoboam took the latter's advice and chose the route of exercising of power and strength—and lost all but two tribes in the rebellion that followed.

When you go on a power trip, be ready to fall. The momentary exhilaration may quickly give way to regret when you experience the fiery reaction.

When the time seemed appropriate, I shared my thoughts with the church leadership team. "I just don't think that fits in this case," responded the most self-assured member of the group. He made his Rehoboam choice, the others went along with him—and the congregation suffered Rehoboam-like consequences.

Leaders need to manage their power and authority. I've already mentioned that I believe authority is the force of presence not the presence of force. Growing up, I heard the phrase, "Power is like soap: the more you use it, the less you'll have."

At times you may need to "flash your claws" to signal your deep concern and your commitment to a specific course of action. This usually comes at a value-challenged time, when a core value, central tenet, or essential principle is at stake. Or when a person truly is trying to take unfair, unjust advantage of you or a situation. But even in such a case, the claws may flash without inflicting injury.

Where do you experience the temptation to exercise your power in leadership, especially in a time of conflict? How has it worked out for you when you've exercised it? How do you process your power choices? These are not cut-and-dried, simplistic questions with expected responses. The leader's use of power is more art than science. And it is definitely a matter for spiritual reflection and discernment.

49
Confidence and Inadequacy

I had one of my most surprising experiences as a new follower of Jesus when I heard my very competent, dynamic pastor, Jerry Kirk, say, "Until recently, I was plagued by feelings of inadequacy. I never felt I measured up."

I was still in high school and knew very well what inadequacy felt like. I couldn't believe that a highly successful Christian leader might feel the same way.

I've since learned that this is true of many. Most don't discuss or admit it, but the undercurrent is never far from mind. It's given the name Imposter Syndrome.[138]

> This is a psychological pattern where individuals doubt their accomplishments and fear being exposed as a "fraud," despite evidence of their competence. They often attribute success to luck or deception rather than their own abilities. Common signs include persistent self-doubt, feeling unworthy of achievements, and anxiety about being "found out." It's prevalent among high achievers, professionals, and those in competitive environments...[139]

As followers of Jesus, we base our confidence and sense of adequacy on a realistic appraisal of our gifts and abilities (Romans 12:3-8), as well as on the promise of God working in and through us.

> Such is the confidence that we have through Christ toward God. Not that we are sufficient in ourselves to claim anything as coming from us, but our sufficiency is from God, who has made us sufficient to be ministers of a new covenant, not of the letter but of the Spirit. For the letter kills, but the Spirit gives life" (2 Corinthians 3:4-6, ESV).

We should never claim to be self-sufficient; that's why I say we are "soul-sufficient." We offer our best, knowing that the work is completely and ultimately in God's hands.

Inadequacy arises from several sources, some of which are appropriate. We normally think that it comes from comparison to others who seem more competent or talented than we see ourselves to be. But another source is a genuine grasp of the size of a task compared to our readily-apparent limitations. In this case, inadequacy is rooted in reality. But that's only when we leave God out of the equation! God can do more with one smooth stone than we could do with an army. Leaders overcome feelings of inadequacy by reminding themselves of two great truths.

First, we draw strength from God's call. Our trust in the sovereign God means that we are exactly where God wants us, doing just what He wants us to do. We gain confidence from the trust God has shown by putting us in this place at this time.

Second, we know that when God calls, God equips. We can pray with confidence, "Lord, you put me in this situation and you alone can work to make it successful. I walk by faith that you will give me the wisdom and strength to do whatever you want me to do."

50
Competing Values and Matters of Conscience

Leaders get caught in some very difficult situations involving competing values and matters of conscience. On a personal level, you know what you would choose if you had only your personal faith and situation to consider. But how do you respond to these competing values in the corporate boardroom, or in the cafeteria, or in the conference room of a small business?

Let's start by saying that easy answers do not exist! Every situation is different. (Great help, I know!) Nevertheless, a few potent principles involving your spiritual identity, destiny, and kingdom partnership can guide you.

Define Yourself

What do you believe, and why do you believe it?

When we enter areas of tension, it's critically important to respond rather than react, to remain calm rather than get defensive. Our confidence comes from knowing what we believe and why we believe it—and that knowledge provides a framework for processing.

You can find useful books, articles, podcasts, and blogs that provide biblical truth, orthodox theology, and godly thinking on almost any topic or issue that you face. The important thing is to know the theological presuppositions and perspective of your sources. Trusted spiritual leaders and counselors can help guide you to the most useful materials.

You also need to understand not only the particular issue, but also the underlying principles that guide your engagement. Context is crucial. A discussion of morality and leadership, for example, differs within a congregation and a business. Pastoral leaders are bound by the authority of Scripture and church governance. Corporations are bound by bylaws and legal regulations. Wise leaders know the appropriate rules and procedures that apply in their situation.

Our culture, for instance, is in the middle of redefining sexuality at every level. One principle for a non-religious business may involve the distinction between civil rights and moral endorsement. An employer may have scruples about a certain belief or behavior (that is, feelings of doubt or strong convictions concerning the morality or appropriateness of that belief or behavior) but does not hesitate to accept a person's right to their own belief and conduct.

Someone may say, "This is what I believe about this situation, but I also respect that good people have other views. So, let's have a mature discussion about what makes the most sense in our circumstances."

Know Your Boundaries

We've discussed the importance of honoring the boundaries of others but haven't yet said much about honoring your own. Consider a few questions for self-reflection:

Are you clear that you are responsible to others but not for others?

Are you kind to yourself by not over-functioning and not over-working?

Do you monitor and manage your emotional investment in people and projects?

Do you maintain a consistent distinction between work and home so that neither "bleeds" into the other?

When you pay attention to your own boundaries, you develop and maintain the emotional reserves and mental margin to respond thoughtfully and calmly instead of reacting impulsively and defensively. Soul care is most important in times of tension and conflict. That's when your discipline (or lack thereof) reveals itself. You may need to take a soul break. Step away for a brief season of prayer and spiritual input[140] to develop God's perspective on the situation.

Expect Tensions and Conflict

In her book *Believers in Business*, Laura L. Nash presents seven creative tensions that believers often face in business:

Tension 1: The Love for God and the Pursuit of Profit
Tension 2: Love and the Competitive Drive
Tension 3: People Needs and Profit Obligations
Tension 4: Humility and the Ego of Success
Tension 5: Family and Work
Tension 6: Charity and Wealth
Tension 7: Faithful Witness in the Secular City [141]

I commend both her book and discussion on each of these issues. My purpose here is to recognize that these are just a few of the issues leaders face. They are part and parcel of living in a world where people, businesses, and corporations try to accomplish something despite their vastly different perspectives (and to be candid, their hang-ups and hurts). It's a miracle we see as much success as we do! That's why we need to accept that struggle is part of the process.

Prepare for Struggle and Responsible Compromise

"What do I do about doubtful practices in my profession in my country?" a public health physician asked her colleagues. "Do I join with them?" What an unsettling question!

Mollie Batten, principal of William Temple College in Manchester, England, replied, "Rarely will the choice be between good and evil. It will be a decision between alternatives, both of which are *partly* good and *partly* evil." And she added: "Insofar as it is for the layman to make a decision and to act upon it, insofar as they make mistakes… God will accept their recognition of this, forgive them, and give them power to try again. This is our faith."

These questions, which sound as contemporary as today's news, come from a series of meetings hosted by the World Council of Churches Assembly at New Delhi in November 1961.[142]

Dr. Batten also remarked:

There will be many occasions on which the layman has to make up his mind whether, in the particular circumstances with which he is confronted, the time has come to make the crucial stand, or to wait and fight another day. I think we have to learn from Jesus Christ that there are many occasions on which the right thing to do is to wait, in order to remain in the situation. When the final stand has to be made, then we must remember that we are called to witness to the greatest power structure in the world, the kingdom of God. "The light shines in the dark, and the darkness has never quenched it" (John 1:5, NEB).[143]

Jesus' followers must learn to master the art of "responsible compromise." This does not require "caving in" to sin and evil. One of the principles that guided my colleagues and me through many a church controversy was "Good and godly people can disagree agreeably." This is not usually comfortable, but it is reality.

Scripture brims over with conflicts and people living in tension, especially in the churches of the New Testament. Consider an extensive quote from Paul's counsel to the Romans:

> Accept other believers who are weak in faith, and don't argue with them about what they think is right or wrong. For instance, one person believes it's all right to eat anything. But another believer with a sensitive conscience will eat only vegetables. Those who feel free to eat anything must not look down on those who don't. And those who don't eat certain foods must not condemn those who do, for God has accepted them. Who are you to condemn someone else's servants? Their own master will judge whether they stand or fall. And with the Lord's help, they will stand and receive his approval.
>
> In the same way, some think one day is more holy than another day, while others think every day is alike. You should each be fully convinced that whichever day you choose is acceptable. Those who worship the Lord on a special day do it to honor him. Those who eat any kind of food do so to honor the Lord, since they give thanks to God before eating. And those who refuse to eat certain foods also want to please the Lord and give thanks to God. For we don't live for ourselves or die for ourselves. If we live, it's to honor the Lord. And if we die, it's to honor the Lord. So whether we live or die, we belong to the Lord. Christ died and rose again for this very purpose—to be Lord both of the living and of the dead. (Romans 14:1-9, NLT).

Sometimes, of course, we must openly protest, or offer our resignation, or even risk our financial well-being. Carefully evaluate these more radical actions with the help and support of wise advisors and counselors. More often than not, you will be called to be salt and light in the middle of these tensions which are inevitable problems of a fallen, in-process-of-being-redeemed world.

I have often drawn strength from the sober assessment of Charles Spurgeon, who back in the nineteenth century wrote, "Trust in God alone, and lean not on the reeds of human help. Be not surprised when friends fail you: it is a failing world. Never count upon immutability in man(sic); inconstancy you may reckon upon without fear of disappointment."[144]

51
Realize It or Not,
You Are a Witness

People watch you. They make assumptions. They draw conclusions. They fill in the blanks. The wise thing to do, then, is to "control the narrative."

As you partner with God and others, look for opportunities to demonstrate intentionally what you believe, what you value, and how much you care about others.

Realize that Most People Have Designed God Out of Their Lives

Most people are not interested in, or even aware of, the Gospel. Most are locked into what philosopher Charles Taylor calls "an immanent frame."[145] As I already mentioned in Chapter 32, we need to remember that most people are "no longer bothered by 'the God question' as a question, because they are devoted to 'exclusive humanism'—a way of being-in-the-world that offers significance without transcendence. They don't feel like anything is missing."[146]

This implies that most individuals probably won't raise questions about the meaning of life. So, says Professor James K.A. Smith (commenting on Taylor's assertion),

> They don't have any sense that the "secular" lives they've constructed are missing a second floor. In many ways, they have constructed webs of meaning that provide almost all the significance they need in their lives (though a lot hinges on that *"almost"*).

> Suffice it to say that the paradigms you brought to your ministry [*or secular business world*] have failed to account for your experience thus far. You thought you were moving to a world like yours, just minus God; but in fact, you've moved to a different world entirely. It turns out this isn't like the Mars Hill of Saint Paul's experience (in Acts 17) where people are devoted to all kinds of deities and you get to add to their pantheon by talking about the

one, true God. No, it seems that many have managed to construct a world of significance that isn't at all bothered by questions of the divine—though that world might still be haunted in some ways, haunted by that *"almost."*[147]

Make People Curious

The world has changed—radically! People are not necessarily concerned with the ultimate questions that greatly interested previous generations. Why not? Because our world has become so disconnected from transcendence that people have become totally absorbed by the here and now, the material world of their experience. Our great hope is that those around us are at least haunted by the "almost" of which Taylor speaks.

We can live in a way that makes people curious. Our relationships with them form the foundation and create the possibility for sharing our faith. "To be a witness does not consist in engaging in propaganda or in stirring people up. It means to live in such a way that one's life would not make sense if God did not exist," said Emmanuel Célestin Cardinal Suhard, Archbishop of Paris (1940–1949).[148]

How can you make your colleagues and your team curious? In part, you can talk about what's going on in your life outside of work: your experience attending a church retreat, or about a sermon (message) you heard on the weekend, by sharing your experience doing a service project, or how your kids are at camp, or a book you're reading. You can also make them curious by how you respond under pressure, or how you express frustration and anger. Some prayerful, creative reflection (especially as part of your Preview discipline) will generate more ideas than you can imagine. I like the following challenge attributed to the Scottish pastor and professor James Stewart:

> If we can but show the world that being committed to Christ is no tame, humdrum, sheltered monotony, but the most thrilling, exciting adventure the human spirit can ever know, those who have been standing outside the church and looking askew at Christ will come crowding in to pay allegiance, and we might well expect the greatest revival since Pentecost.[149]

It is and always has been a challenge to grow continually in the experience of faith. Far too easily we can fall into apathy and indifference unless we intentionally engage to develop our spiritual vitality.

Explain Your Values and the Rationale for Your Decisions

At times you can explain why you have made some recommendation or decision. At other times you can invite people into the process with you.

I have often opened a conversation like this: "Let me bring you into my dilemma…" I then state the issues and conflicting values as clearly as possible and begin the dialogue. This makes it easier to share the principles that undergird your actions and decisions.

I encourage the leaders that I coach to keep a running list of insights and principles that they accumulate through their experience. Some will be original with them, while others are tried and true wisdom confirmed by their experience. The point is to understand and articulate why we do what we do. This practice adds depth to our engagement and credibility to our leadership.

52

A Rowing Partnership or a Sailing Partnership?

We all know what it's like to do a group project when one or two group members drop the ball and fail to carry their share of the weight. Those of us who care about the outcome then pick up the slack. We row extra hard to ensure the boat crosses the finish line. Nevertheless, we resent the leeches who take their share of the credit without carrying their share of the load.

That's one of the problems with a rowing strategy! We don't respect our own boundaries, and we shield ourselves and others from failure. We think we have no choice, but actually, we do. We can choose to do our part and let others see the "gaps" created by those who don't contribute. Of course, the higher the value, the riskier the consequences of "limiting" our work!

A sailing partnership, by contrast, relies on the wind of the Spirit and the crew God has given us. That's risky—but so is rowing in high seas. It's not easy to rely on others!

I'll always remember a college basketball coach who declared, "It's really difficult to watch a nineteen-year-old run up and down the court with your paycheck in his mouth!" The success of the coach depends on the success of the players. It's the same with all leaders.

But stop and think about this: *It's the same with the Lord*.

A famous story tells how Jesus, after the cross and the resurrection, returned to his glory, still bearing the marks of his sufferings.

An angel said to him, "You must have suffered terribly for people down there."

"I did," said Jesus.

"Do they all know about what you did for them?" asked the angel.

"No," said Jesus, "not yet. Only a few in Israel know about it so far."

"What have you done that they should all know about it?" the angel wondered.

"Well," said Jesus, "I asked Peter and James and John to make it their business to tell others, and then others tell still others, until the farthest person on the widest circle has heard the story."

The angel looked doubtful, for he knew well what poor creatures people were. "Yes," he said, "but what if Peter and James and John forget? What if they grow weary of the telling? What if, way down in the twentieth century, people fail to tell the story of your love for them? What then? Haven't you made any other plans?"

"I haven't made any other plans," Jesus responded. "I'm counting on them."

Jesus died to give us the gospel; and now he is counting on *us* to transmit it to everyone else.[150]

We are God's Plan A. There is no Plan B.

In the case of the group project illustration mentioned above, soul-sailors take time to clarify every person's responsibility, ensure that everyone has the resources they need, and then monitor their process to be sure each person is moving forward with the team. All the while, they pray and seek God's direction, trusting God's provision.

Can things still go wrong? Of course! But failure isn't fatal.

Spiritually healthy leaders learn to keep the big picture in mind, so they don't overreact to smaller problems. It takes only a few of these "failures" to either stimulate change in the under-performing team members or to be able to move them to positions better suited for their temperament and skills. And yes, that may mean termination. But even that we entrust to God. One of my good friends, Wally Upton, used to say, "It's a sin to keep a person in a job where they're failing."

God cares more about his will being done and his kingdom coming "on earth as it is in heaven" than we do. God loves us and our neighbors to an extent we can never fathom. And when we join the Lord in this glorious work, we know that our labor is never in vain (see 1 Corinthians 15:58).

53
Spiritual Disciplines Keep Your Inner Game of Partnership Alive

The disciplines of Presence and Purpose help leaders stay connected to the Lord, their kingdom partner, in the thick of business. In particular, the discipline of Preview is one of the most practical exercises to cultivate God's presence moment-by-moment.

All three disciplines of Purpose (Calling, Character, and Community) will help keep you centered and thriving in your context.

Let's begin with Preview. Let me add a bit to what I described about Preview in Chapter 38.

Stay Connected with God Throughout the Day

It's easy for leaders to forget all about God when they get swept along in the swift current of daily events and responsibilities. But it's not inevitable! You can learn to use events to turn your attention to the Lord.

I told the following story in my book *SoulShaping (Second Edition)*,[151] but it's worth summarizing here.

In the first congregation I served as an associate pastor, I led a weekly Bible study of men. We met in the early morning in Old Greenwich, Connecticut, and then the men caught a train to Grand Central Station in New York City.

One morning, a man I'll call Jim suggested we change from meeting in the morning to meeting at noon for lunch in midtown Manhattan, one time each month. I said I would certainly consider the idea but wondered why he wanted to make the shift.

"This study is really helpful," Jim began, "but to be honest, by the time I get to my office, I have pretty much forgotten what we studied and discussed. I have a feeling that if I had an appointment for a Bible study on my calendar midday, I'd think more about God throughout that day."

Jim's comment about his calendar sparked an idea. After we discussed his proposal, I said, "Let's do something different for our closing prayer. Get out your calendars (this took place before mobile phones). Take some time to pray over each of your appointments and 'to do' lists. Picture the Lord with you in every situation. After you pray, put a cross, a Bible verse, or any idea that comes to you in prayer by that appointment or 'to do' item. Then, when you look at your schedule during the day, you will think of the Lord and this prayer time."

God worked in an amazing way in Jim's life that day, a story I tell more fully in my previous book. But for now, I want to encourage you to pray expectantly over your calendar, every day, with a listening heart and creative imagination.

God's Purpose Directs Our Steps[152]

Spiritual disciplines equip us to live, work, serve, and play to the fullest. They are means, not ends. They enable us to draw life from the Lord so we can serve God's purposes in this world.

Spirituality is not just about feeling good. Spirituality is about living well. As God's partners, we continually condition ourselves to develop spiritual stamina and the qualities of a life marked by the fruit of God's Spirit.

We represent Christ and model Christian values to everyone with whom we interact. We cannot separate who we are from how we conduct our lives. That's why I see character as a spiritual discipline. We cultivate a character discipline by that moment-by-moment awareness that every choice shapes us. We look at every decision in terms of eternity, not expediency. We consider every choice in terms of reputation, not immediate satisfaction. In terms of integrity, not pleasure.

I learned this the hard way regarding my anger. I usually controlled my anger, but early in my ministry got ambushed by my feelings. At one elder meeting (we Presbyterians call it "Session"), we were struggling with a tough decision when one elder, whom I had counted as an ally and friend, suddenly called for "The Order of the Day." I asked what he meant.

"Our standing rules call for mandatory adjournment of the session by 10:00 p.m.," he answered. It was 9:58 p.m. He seemed uncharacteristically harsh, antagonistic, and angry.

I felt trapped, cornered. For the first time I can remember, I literally saw red. I was furious! My heart was pounding, my chest tightened, and my vision was tinged with crimson.

Even today, I can hardly believe how quickly it happened. I tried to suppress my feelings, but they insisted on spilling out.

I didn't even know the Session had such a policy—and that elder had done a *lot* of the talking at that meeting. I wanted to lash out.

"It doesn't seem fair to raise that issue like this, at the last minute," I said. "You yourself have talked a great deal during our meeting and we still have a few essential decisions to make."

I knew immediately that although I had voiced a correct observation, I would pay a price in our relationship.

The elders could see the stunned look on my face, and mercifully, they began to negotiate to "extend the docket." I won't bore you with details, but they persuaded the majority to extend the meeting by fifteen minutes. The elder who had raised the protest cast the only dissenting vote, then got up and walked out in a huff. Things were never the same between us.

That night I learned the hard truth that leaders must control their anger. I frequently quote the saying, "Anger and criticism are like mud: they brush off much better when they're dry."

Leaders take character seriously because they take their call in Christ seriously.

God's Call Marks Every Aspect of Our Lives

Leaders also cultivate a clear sense of call. I distinguish two aspects of call: our daily call as disciples and our vocational call to make our ultimate contribution to God's coming kingdom.

Our most basic call is to be living reminders[153] of Jesus Christ by the way we live each moment. Being a "living reminder" is not as abstract as it sounds. We reveal Jesus' presence by how we care for hurting people. We can serve as a quiet conscience in times of decision. We exercise ethical influence in leadership, model hope in discouragement, and witness to recovery in brokenness. That's what it looks like to "deny ourselves and take up our cross daily and follow Jesus" (see Luke 9:23). It's not a formula; it's a way of living.

So, we begin our day saying, "I am yours, Lord. Fill my sails with your Holy Spirit." Then we preview our day with prayer and spiritual imagination. And then we pay attention, watching for how God moves around us.

The second aspect of calling invites us to frame our leadership and career in light of our ultimate contribution to life. We already discussed this concept in our section on Destiny.[154] The disciplines around vocational calling concern themselves with keeping first things first.

While you have many responsibilities, the important thing to remember is that how you do what you do matters as much as what you *actually* do. That includes how you love your neighbors in both your family and career contexts.

In Community You Create Safe Places for Health and Growth

Partnership, by necessity, involves more than one person, which means it necessitates community. But we live in a culture experiencing deep isolation and loneliness.

In his book, *Bowling Alone*, Harvard Professor Robert Putnam explores the thesis that life as we enter the new millennium differs greatly from life in the 1950s. He's primarily concerned with what he calls the significant loss of "social capital."

> Whereas physical capital refers to physical objects and human capital refers to properties of individuals, social capital refers to connections among individuals—social networks and the norms of reciprocity and trustworthiness that arise from them.[155]

Naturally, we may ask, "So what? What's the big deal?" Putnam replies,

> What is at stake is not merely warm, cuddly feelings or *frissons* [French word for "intense excitement"] of community pride. We shall review hard evidence that our schools and neighborhoods don't work so well when community bonds slacken, that our economy, our democracy, and even our health and happiness depend on adequate stocks of social capital.[156]

Loving our neighbors as ourselves lies at the heart of our faith. But the satisfying experience of relationships can be hit-or-miss if we lack a vision for the quality of community God desires for us.

Paul gives an expansive description of healthy community:

> Put on then, as God's chosen ones, holy and beloved, compassionate hearts, kindness, humility, meekness, and patience, bearing with one another and, if one has a complaint against another, forgiving each other; as the Lord has forgiven you, so you also must forgive. And above all these put on love, which binds everything together in perfect harmony. And let the peace of Christ rule in your hearts, to which indeed you were called in one body. And be thankful. Let the word of Christ

dwell in you richly, teaching and admonishing one another in all wisdom, singing psalms and hymns and spiritual songs, with thankfulness in your hearts to God. And whatever you do, in word or deed, do everything in the name of the Lord Jesus, giving thanks to God the Father through him (Colossians 3:12-17, ESV).

Such a quality of community is not automatic. It requires intentional nurturing by individuals who are both humble and grateful. Those who experience this type of community thrive.

Leaders set the tone for their communities, for the relational interactions with the individuals and teams around them. That's why leaders must take time to care. Even very simple practices can help weave the bonds that strengthen teams.

I suggest that when you begin a meeting, start with acknowledging relational connections like this: "Before we tackle our agenda, I just want to say that [Diane] told me I could share that her husband is in the hospital. She really appreciates your thoughts and prayers. Does anyone else have anything to share before we get started?" Such a simple beginning is not a waste of time; it is weaving the fabric of a community that will work more efficiently and effectively together because they care.

Never in Your Own Energy

We began with a quote from A. W. Tozer that said, "Your work in the world is sacred." Now you have a sense of what that work looks like.

In one sense, it's quite simple: be a living reminder of Jesus in all you say and do. That task becomes complex, however, if you try to do it in your own energy. But, remember, you were never meant to do so!

Pull in your oars and put up your sail. Watch with joy as the Lord takes you through both calm seas and rough waters. Rejoice that *you* get to be part of and partner with the coming kingdom of God.

Part Five

Fill My Sails, Lord

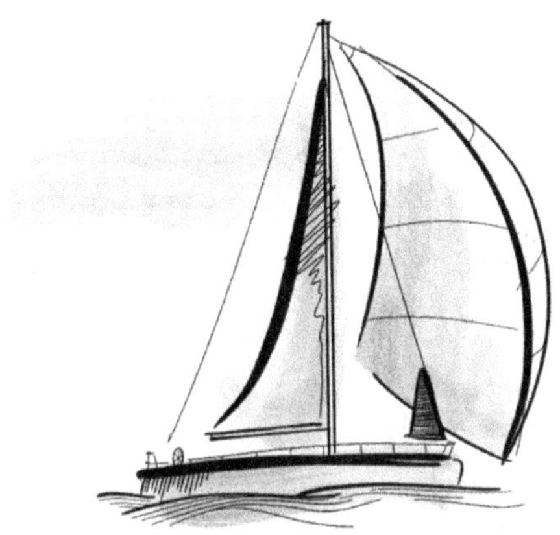

Lasting impact and joyful living flow from understanding
your identity
your destiny
and your partnership in Christ.

This approach to leadership and to life frees you from both externally-imposed and internally-generated pressures. You cultivate a disciple/student/learning posture and attitude. You grow in your skill of framing your positive and negative experiences in terms of your identity, destiny, and partnership mission.

When you shape your life with this spiritual meaning, motivation, and mindset, your soul grows in stability, confidence, and unwavering trust in God. Life becomes an adventure when every day, every situation, every relationship becomes an opportunity to see God move.

*Everyone then who hears these words of mine and does them
will be like a wise man who built his house upon the rock;
and the rain fell, and the floods came,
and the winds blew and beat upon that house, but it did not fall,
because it had been founded on the rock.*

—JESUS, IN MATTHEW 7:24-25 (RSV)

*No horse gets anywhere till he's harnessed,
no steam drives anything until it's confined,
no Niagara ever turned anything into light or power until it's tunneled,
no life ever grows great until focused, dedicated and disciplined.*

—HARRY EMERSON FOSDICK[157]

*We do not think ourselves into a new way of living;
we live ourselves into a new way of thinking.*

—RICHARD ROHR[158]

*Do all the good you can, in all the ways you can, to all the souls you can,
in every place you can, at all the times you can, with all the zeal you can as
long as ever you can.*

—JOHN WESLEY, ATTRIBUTED[159]

If within us we find nothing over us, we succumb to what is around us.

—P. T. FORSYTH, ATTRIBUTED[160]

54
Life's Biggest Questions Answered

The goal of this book has been to provide reasonable, biblical responses to life's essential questions so that leaders can experience the most significant and satisfying life possible. We've considered three primary questions, viewing them in the context of Jesus' final moments with His disciples in the Upper Room. Let's reflect on his situation one more time:

> Jesus, knowing that the Father had given all things into his hands, and that he had come from God and was going back to God, rose from supper. He laid aside his outer garments, and taking a towel, tied it around his waist. Then he poured water into a basin and began to wash the disciples' feet and to wipe them with the towel that was wrapped around him (John 13:3-5, ESV).

Who Tells Me Who I Am?

Our identity is the foundation for meaning in life. Start with who you are in Christ. If you allow the world's values to define you, you will be driven on a relentless search for more. If you seek to define yourself, you will fall into pride, arrogance, and most often, disillusionment.

Jesus' identity was reflected in the fact that he knew he "that he had come from God." He knew he was one with the Father and continually nurtured that connection. He lived, served, died, rose from the dead, and ascended to heaven in the unwavering knowledge of his identity.

God alone gives us our true identity. It's theologically appropriate to imagine hearing the words God spoke to Jesus at his baptism spoken also to you, "You are my beloved child. I am very pleased with you!" You are God's child, a member of God's family, a joint heir with Jesus Christ (see Romans 8:14-15). Marinate in these truths so they permeate every fiber of your consciousness and influence every aspect of your being. These truths change everything.

And you are not only God's child, but you are also God's partner in his "Family Business" of bringing his Kingdom on earth as it is in heaven. This is the basis for our response to life's second big question.

What Is Life's Real Bottom Line?

Your destiny fuels your motivation in life. Your destiny looks beyond the horizon of this world. Stephen Covey taught the importance of the principle, "Begin with the end in mind." Place this phrase in the eternal context: "Begin with The End—your death and resurrection hope—in mind."

Jesus not only knew he had come from God (his identity), but he also knew "that he was going back to God" (John 13:3)—that was his destiny. His entire life focused on his earthly mission and his eternal destiny. He articulated his earthly mission in many ways, but perhaps he spoke the most succinct and comprehensive statement when he said, "the Son of Man came not to be served but to serve, and *to give his life as a ransom for many*" (Mark 1:45, ESV, emphasis added).

We know that as followers of Jesus we have passed from death to life. We also know that our work in this life will be evaluated (1 Corinthians 3:11-15). This eternal perspective helps us redeem our time, shape our priorities, and clarify our values. It also purifies and directs our ambition. We live in the moment, but not for the moment. We see every moment in light of its eternal significance. We know that, like Jesus, we are to give our lives to serve God's purposes. That is the basis for our response to life's third big question.

What Is God's Will for My Life?

Partnership frames our mindset for life. God's will and purpose for your life can be framed in many ways, but our primary understanding is that God calls us into relationship with him as disciples and as partners in his kingdom work. You engage in your work as God's partner in the continuing work of Jesus and his kingdom in this world.

Leaders often ask me, "How do I take my faith into the workplace and marketplace?" You start by realizing your faith is not a commodity separate from you. You don't "take" your faith anywhere. You *are* your faith. You *are* a disciple. You *are* a partner with God. You simply need to learn to be who you already are.

Simply? When I say "simply," I realize there's nothing simple about it, at least at first. I remember when my wife and I first began teaching our children to swim while they were still very young. The instructor started by having us hold them on their backs to learn to float. And what did our children do? All four of them curled up in a ball, tight as could be! They couldn't relax and float. It took time and trust to learn to relax and float.

Time and trust.

Learning to rest in the Lord and be the person he calls you to be takes time and trust. By practicing intentional exposure to the Living Water, you learn to trust that God's got not only the whole world in his hands, but also your individual life, in his loving, omnipotent hands. You learn to rest, to relax, to float by faith. To sail by faith.

Knowing that he had come from God and was returning to God, Jesus vividly demonstrated the nature of his partnership with God by washing the disciples' feet. Jesus not only would fulfill his mission, but through the whole experience, he would also preserve and care for those devastated and tested beyond their limits.

In a culture preoccupied with power, personal choice, options, and entitlement, Jesus sounded a dissonant chord of role reversal. Jesus, the Master, played the role of servant. Jesus, the Lord of Light, plunged into the depths of darkness. Jesus, the Sinless One, became sin for us.

And he enacted this paradox in his prophetic actions during his final hours.

We deliberately imitate Jesus' posture as servant leaders. We show our neighbors God's love in practical ways. We know that *how* we do what we do is as important as what we do. We may not do different things, but we do everything differently. We live the paradox of servant leadership: using our position and power to serve the needs of our teams, our clients, and our customers. We aren't in it for the perquisites ("perks"). It's not about the rewards; it's about the responsibility.

Like Jesus, you are called to serve in the work of God's coming kingdom, knowing that your greatest reward is giving glory to God.

A Rooted Response

Our responses to these three essential questions are all rooted in John 13:3-15.

> *Identity*—Jesus knew he had come from God. The dove descending at his baptism symbolizes this.

> *Destiny*—Jesus knew he was returning to God. We can symbolize this as his crown, ruling from his eternal throne.

Partnership—Jesus washed his disciples' feet. The pitcher, basin, and towel he used symbolize this.

Such an approach to leadership—and to life—frees you from externally-imposed and internally-generated pressures. You cultivate a disciple/student/learning posture and attitude. You grow in your skill of framing your positive and negative experiences in terms of your identity, destiny, and partnership mission.

What happens when you fail? You claim your identity in Christ and say, "This failure does not define me." Claiming your destiny in Christ, you say, "This failure is part of life in a fallen world with fallen human beings. In the light of eternity, I trust God to redeem it as part of His plan." Claiming your partnership in Christ, you say, "Lord, unless You build the house, I will labor in vain. But I know that You continue to work, and I continue to be available to you."

Do you see how easily you can use this framing mindset for success, too? When you succeed, in terms of your identity you say, "This success does not define me." In terms of your destiny, you say, "This success is a sign of God's grace and mercy in this fallen world. In the light of eternity, the greatest value of this success is furthering God's work." In terms of your partnership, you say, "Lord, thank you for the privilege of working with you. My greatest joy is being part of your continuing work in this world."

55
What Could God Do Through You?

Too easily we tend to accept the status quo and accommodate our expectations to its limitations. But we serve a God who can do more in a moment than we can accomplish in a lifetime.

Looking back over what God has done in the past can stimulate your vision for the future. In the second century, Diognetus described the fledgling Christian community that he observed:

> They dwell in their country, but simply as sojourners. As citizens, they share things as if foreigners. Every foreign land is to them as their native country, and every country of their birth as a land of strangers. They marry, as do all others; they beget children; but they do not destroy their offspring. They have a common table not a common bed. They are in the flesh, but do not live after the flesh. They pass their days on earth, but they are citizens of heaven. They obey the prescribed laws and at the same time surpass the laws by their lives. They love all men and are persecuted by all. They are unknown and condemned; they are put to death and restored to life. They are poor yet make many rich; they are in lack of all things yet abound in all; they are dishonored and yet in their very dishonor are glorified. They are evil spoken of and yet are justified; they are reviled and bless; they are insulted and repay the insult with honor; they do good, yet are punished as evil-doers. When punished, they rejoice as if quickened into life; they are assailed by the Jews as foreigners and are persecuted by the Greeks; yet those who hate them are unable to assign any reason for their hatred.[161]

Frost and Hirsch conclude this description with the comment, "Even those who don't share our faith will be impressed with so loving and gracious a community." Don't you agree?

So, what's *your* inspiring vision? It may help to start by considering where you are most disappointed and discouraged. Take a few moments for intentional reflection and meditation. Fold a sheet of paper in half lengthwise or make two vertical columns on a computer document. On the left side put the heading "What I See Now" and write some specific points that cause you the most concern. Then, on the right side, put "What God Could Do" and generate some ideas and dreams for what God may do in your situation. By faith, God begins to move when we fill our minds with what God could do. This is one aspect of what it means to walk by faith, not by sight (see 2 Corinthians 5:7).

You may be new to living in this way, but God has been at this sort of thing for a very long time. Nearly three hundred years ago, England had descended into a period of spiritual malaise and indifference. Deism had become the dominant religion of the day. Deists saw God as something like a brilliant but disinterested clockmaker, who wound up the universe, set it running on natural laws, and then ceased any ongoing connection with it.

However, as always, God preserved a remnant of faithful followers who could bring a spark of revival (see 1 Kings 19:18). One such person was Lady Huntingdon, who knew both John Wesley, founder of Methodism, and his protégé, George Whitefield.[162]

Lady Huntingdon felt deeply troubled by her nation's sinful condition. "But Lord," she prayed, "what am I to do about it? My generation lies lost in darkness. They're like sheep without a shepherd. God, may you pour abundant blessings upon our sinful country and help me to fill my place in your work."[163]

She had lost her husband at age thirty-nine to a stroke and then lost two of her four children to smallpox. Rather than falling into bitterness, she rose in her passion to share the hope of the gospel with her friends. One day, when Whitefield returned to England between visits to the American colonies, she proposed a partnership of sorts.

God chose me to be a member of England's nobility," she told him, "and now I'm ready to use my position for Jesus' sake. I have a burden for the influential in England. They won't go out to the fields to hear Methodist preachers, and when they attend church, they hear sermons with no theological guts. Whitefield, I want you to bring the gospel to them—in my home, starting tomorrow night.[164]

Their strategy became one of the most effective means of stirring revival in the 18th century.

This model of in-home, relationship-based groups can be used in a variety of ways to share the gospel and lead people into deeper discipleship.[165] In Lady Huntingdon's case, it came about through a combination of deep-felt need and inspired religious creativity.

Leaders stimulate holy imagination. When I served as lead pastor at the First Presbyterian Church of Fresno, California, we wanted to purchase the city block across the street from our campus. We owned a very small corner of that block, using it for about twenty-five parking places. We needed most of the block, however, for parking on Sundays. If we lost that parking, we would have a very hard time.

When we tried to purchase the property, we learned that half of it was jointly owned by several parties—who were all serving jail time for fraud! Our efforts met with frustration and delay. I felt an intense urgency to resolve this situation. So, at the conclusion of one sermon, I said to the congregation, "Right now, that piece of property across the street seems to be locked up, out of our reach. I invite each of you parked on that parcel of ground to pray that God would unlock the chains for us so that his name will be glorified! Let's do a 'Jericho Walk' around the property and see if the walls of resistance will tumble down."

After both worship services, I felt gratified to see whole families, singles in groups, individuals, couples—nearly everyone—literally walking all the way around the block, stopping to pray at various places. Some held hands in a circle to pray, others just walked. What a blessing to see such a concrete expression of support!

Eight days later … we owned the block! (That's another story.)

Leaders help others push through obstacles. They encourage hope when their team feels defeated. They inspire courage when their people feel intimidated. They take time to help team members to dare to dream again.

You can do the same thing. Why not?

56
What I Learned From My Day in Court

One morning as I walked down the halls of the Orange County Justice Center, I saw a member of our congregation. Rodger, a defense attorney, asked me why I was there. Feeling playful, I said, "Go ahead and guess."

"The most obvious is jury duty," he said.

"Nope."

"Are you a witness in a case?"

"Nope."

"Are you going to small claims court?"

"Nope."

"I give up. Seriously, why are you here??"

"I'm here because Judge Kim in our congregation invited me to shadow her for the day."

He smiled broadly and replied, "Well, that's amazing! Get ready, because you're going to see things you are *not* used to seeing!"

My invitation came after I preached a series of sermons on the topics of this book. I had encouraged church members to invite me to work. And Judge Kim wrote me the following email:

Dear Doug,

I wanted to see if you would like to come to my court and watch a morning or afternoon session to get a feel for what we really do in the criminal arena. I run a large criminal calendar, and you would have an opportunity to see how we help people, many of whom have struggled their whole lives, in their moment of crisis.

It is a humbling experience to work in this field because it constantly reminds me that "But for the grace of God that could be me." That realization strikes you every day sitting in a court like mine. It reminds me daily that we are all the same: sinners.

I get the privilege of talking to prostitutes, drug addicts, alcoholics, abusers, sexual deviants, thieves, and many other criminals every day. It is really enlightening and the only difference between most of them and the "rest of us" is that their sins are crimes.

Signed,
Kim

I sat behind the judge's clerks in the courtroom, watching an amazing series of "mini dramas" unfold. If I remember correctly, Judge Kim processed sixty-four cases that day. Some were assigned to open courts "forthwith!" Others were scheduled for future dates. And some were resolved right then and there.

I was pleasantly surprised to see the amount of pastoral care coming from the thoughtful, conscientious members of the justice system. I watched Judge Kim dialogue with defendants pleading guilty. She took the time to ask them what they had learned from this experience and what they would do differently in the future. She laughed, she taught, she "chastised." I watched her advise people of their rights and urge them to think through their legal options. I watched her work with attorneys who advocated for the accused.

As we spoke at lunch with another judge, it became very clear that Kim understood this as her ministry. She brought her faith into all her interactions.

Because that's what kingdom partners do.

57
You Need Double Vision

When I played trumpet (and later French horn) in school bands and orchestras, we learned to pay attention both to reading our music and to watching the conductor out of the corner of our eye. It wasn't enough to be locked in on the music, nor to rivet our attention on the conductor. We needed to divide our attention to produce a unified performance.

We needed a type of double vision.

It's the same in leadership. We need to focus on the compelling vision we are called to execute by virtue of our position, and, at the same time, keep the corner of our eye on God, our Holy Conductor. We want to do God's work God's way, even in jobs and projects that are not overtly "religious" or spiritual.

We do this by taking the extra step of praying over our work, as with the discipline of Preview. We exercise our holy imagination in prayer to discern how God is working in our situation. We invite God into every meeting, every appointment, every project, every plan, every conflict, every challenge, every temptation, every frustration. This need not be a public declaration but instead can reflect our intentional posture of expectation. We cultivate alertness to where God is moving.

When we face the inevitable conflict, we ask the Lord to "make the rough places level and smooth" (Isaiah 40:4, paraphrase).

When we don't know how to express ourselves, we pray silently, "Holy Spirit, give me the words for this situation" (Luke 12:12, paraphrase). Do not limit your expectations or requests to situations that seem more spiritual or evangelistic to you. You do not know how God will use whatever you say!

When you face a direct attack on your integrity, I'd suggest two steps. First, call on the Lord to reveal anything you need to hear that could give instruction, something like David's prayer:

Search me, O God, and know my heart!
Try me and know my thoughts!

And see if there be any grievous way in me,
and lead me in the way everlasting (Psalm 139:23-24, ESV).

Second, call on the Lord for protection and vindication, praying, "Lord, protect me from those who are out to get me. I trust you to protect me, my reputation, and all you have entrusted to me. I am eagerly watching for how you will work" (Psalm 27:11-14, paraphrase).

No doubt you can see how this holy exercise could go on and on as you consider specific circumstances. But the point is not to catalogue a series of situations and responses (as valuable an exercise as that might be) but to develop holy reflexes that shape spiritually mature responses to all life's challenges.

These holy reflexes develop by paying attention to the spiritual score that God the composer has given you and by paying attention to God's cues as he conducts you through life. You might even embark on some holy improvisation.

It's double vision with a single result: victory.

58
The Link Between Desire and Achievement

How do you develop such double vision? How do you bridge the gap between desire and achievement? I know of only one way: discipline.

Personal growth in every area of life requires the investment of intentional effort. In general, with youth comes the gift of a healthy body. As we age, however, what we first received as a gift must be maintained and cultivated through discipline, through intentional effort. When cared for with proper nutrition, exercise, and rest our bodies can serve us in strength and in health for many years.

We see a similar principle in the spiritual realm. Newly committed, newly-born followers of Christ often brim over with enthusiasm; some might even call them obnoxious. They can't wait to read the Bible. Every prayer seems to be answered, and they find God at work around every corner.

The time comes, however, when the intensity and immediacy of God's presence diminishes. The maturing believer learns more about the need for personal effort empowered by the Spirit, and about discipline and consistency as factors in spiritual growth.

Physically and spiritually, you can focus on the losses you suffer, or you can learn to focus on your ability to become a responsible agent in your own life and growth. The initial gifts of physical youth and spiritual youth primed the pump, but the mature choices of growth tap the well of Living Waters. It means pulling in your oars and putting up your sails. Taking personal responsibility frees you from the vagaries of circumstances. That is the sign of inner transformation.

Discipline produces the freedom to face life with confidence. Discipline develops "spiritual reflexes" before you need them. Spiritual discipline develops soul memory. You develop spiritual reflexes to respond to life in God's way. You discipline yourself to develop soul memory in normal times so that you'll be equipped for the times of high demand or deep crisis. That is the way to thrive in Jesus.[166]

You exercise discipline in many areas. You exercise discipline to schedule your priorities. You exercise financial discipline to support God's work in a variety of ways and to keep free from excessive debt. You exercise physical discipline to maintain your health and stamina to enjoy life. You exercise mental discipline to continue your intellectual growth and the renewing of your mind in Christ.

At times you also must create space to be "at ease." Sabbath time helps you break from activity addiction and refreshes you both spiritually and physically.[167] Discipline and rest are complimentary, not antithetical! Abundant life in Christ reflects a natural discipline that stewards the gifts, opportunities, and responsibilities God provides without anxiety and care. This is the expression of Jesus' light burden and easy yoke (see Matthew 11:28-30).

Jim Rohn, an American entrepreneur, author, and motivational speaker, said, "We must all suffer from one of two pains: the pain of discipline or the pain of regret. The difference is discipline weighs ounces, while regret weighs tons."[168]

Do you see the real irony here? Those who exercise the least discipline often find themselves under the most pressure.

59
Build Momentum

"If anything is worth doing, it is worth doing poorly."[169] These words from G. K. Chesterton cause most of us to cringe. But the principle he offered is not an excuse for poor effort. Rather, it removes the excuse of perfectionism that often blocks effort.

If some suggestion in this book has seemed good to you, try it just once or for a few days. Start with small steps. Do not, for example, make a commitment to study the Bible for an hour a day for the rest of your life. Commit to reading one verse or one chapter a day for one week and see how that works for you. That's the key to progress.

When I told a friend, Derek, about my work on this book, he replied, "Ugh! I don't like leadership books."

"Well, that's encouraging!" I responded. "What don't you like about them?"

"They're usually overwhelming. When I read them, I feel like I can never measure up to being a good leader."

"But you're doing some amazing things in your ministry," I replied. "I know you're an effective leader."

"That may be true," he said, "but I don't measure up to what I read in most of those books."

I certainly hope this book fits in a different category! So, let me make a few things clear.

Leadership is about *who we are*. It's *not* a series of management techniques by which we micromanage ourselves and others. It's about our *being* in Christ that empowers natural *doing* with Christ. My friend was thinking about leadership as rowing, not as sailing.

The premise of James Clear's book, *Atomic Habits*, is that tiny changes trigger remarkable results. Clear presents the Two Minute rule: "When you start a new habit, it should take less than two minutes to do."[170]

With that in mind, the advice—

"Read before bed each night" becomes "Read one page."

"Study for class" becomes "Open my notes."

"Fold laundry" becomes "Fold one pair of socks."

"Run three miles" becomes "Tie my running shoes."

Once you've started the right thing, it is much easier to keep doing it!

Clear tells how "Mitch" struggled to lose weight. So, Mitch tried the principle of starting with a two-minute goal. He went to the gym each day, but he told himself he couldn't stay for more than five minutes. (He thought five minutes, not two, was the bare minimum for him!) He would arrive at the gym, exercise for five minutes, and leave. After a few weeks, he looked around and thought, *Well, I'm always coming here anyway; I might as well stay a little longer*. Soon he was up to an hour exercise routine. At the same time, he became more intentional about reducing his calorie intake—again, reducing in small steps. Within a few years, Mitch had lost 100 lbs.

The basic message is very simple: You must establish a habit before you can improve it.[171]

Use this approach, at your own pace, to develop leadership momentum. Make one change to your day, such as implementing the discipline of Preview one morning a week before work. Or practice Review at the end of a day. Or consider which concept helps you most: Identity, Destiny, or Partnership. Then slowly reread a page a day from the chapters in that section and journal on them.

The process is the product. You won't arrive at a place called "Leader." Being a leader is experienced in the process of leading. These concepts, when forefront in your mind, generate the mindset that will make your work more significant and satisfying. And it will be *significant* because you'll be incorporating your values and helping others grow in the process. It will be *satisfying* because you'll experience the lifestyle and activities that feel most meaningful to you. You'll honor the dual aspects of leadership in serving others effectively as you experience the goodness and satisfaction of work well done. That's what we mean by lasting impact and joyful living.

60
Don't Try to Go It Alone

Heroic individualism is overrated. It makes for great cinema but flops in real life.

From the beginning, the Lord God said, "It is not good for the man to be alone" (Genesis 2:18, NIV). In this case, God quite literally meant "man" (the male) because he was about to make Adam's female counterpart(ner). God always brings people together for fellowship and service. Think of just a few biblical examples:

Abraham and Sarah
Moses and Joshua
Naomi and Ruth
David and his mighty men
Mary and Elizabeth
Jesus and the disciples
Paul and Timothy
Priscilla and Aquilla

Leaders need safe relationships in which they can wrestle through their personal, career, and business challenges. Appropriate levels of disclosure exist based on the nature of the relationship.

Dual relationships always present a challenge: the situation when you're a friend but also have an official (usually supervisory role) with that person. Think of friendship between a professor and a student, a doctor and a patient, a boss and an employee, even a pastor and a church leader. Each relationship is unique and must be managed with wisdom and sensitivity to the appropriate dynamics. Often, these are not the ideal contexts for truly safe relationships of vulnerability and disclosure.

You likely will find safety in relationships with peers who are not directly involved in your vocational life. A gathering of executives from different business sectors can bring perspective and provide a rich forum for empathetic sharing and understanding. They "get it" in terms of employees, board members, and cultural and regulatory pressures.

Likewise, a group of employees from different companies can gather and relate to one another with appropriate empathy and vulnerability.

All relationships and groups should follow basic guidelines for confidential sharing. The most important guideline is, "What is shared in the group is not shared outside the group." The first time someone violates that group confidentiality, it ceases to be a safe place. The results can devastate, but the temptation is always present because information is power. We can feel tempted to make ourselves seem more important if we are somehow "in the know" with an important person. But we will lose that privilege if we violate that person's trust.

I've always made it a priority to be in a small group with men I can trust. I'm still in one to this day. It's a group of three other men who keep me anchored, who pray for me, and support me. I do the same for them. We're there for each other. Yes, we do go through seasons when we hold back from each other, usually without fully realizing it. But then one of us will challenge the group, "Hey, what's really going on in your life? What do you want to celebrate? Where are you really struggling? Let's get down to it." And we do.

This concept also applies to our overall approach to collaboration and teamwork. Leaders build teams. Leaders take time for relationships. These don't have to be "deep" relationships in which sharing is the predominant purpose. But leaders make relationships a priority and take time to value people in the middle of performing tasks.

61
The Cost of Carelessness

It's hard to watch an imminent collision when you lack the power to do anything to prevent it. As they say, you can see the train wreck coming.

Leaders are not guaranteed a strong finish. In fact, as noted earlier, Professor Bobby Clinton claims that less than thirty percent of leaders whose final days are recorded in the Bible finished well. As we read through many of the accounts of the kings of Judah (the southern kingdom in the line of King David), we want to cry out, "Don't do it! Don't go there! You're headed for disaster!" But off they go.

King Uzziah (also called Azariah), a very successful king, ruled for fifty-two years at a prosperous time in Judah's history. "But when he became powerful, he became proud, which led to his downfall" (2 Chronicles 26:16, NLT). He presumptuously attempted to burn incense in the temple—a privilege permitted solely to the priests—and God struck him with leprosy. Because of his uncleanness, he lived in isolation until the day he died.

We ask ourselves, "*What* was he thinking? Uzziah had everything he could possibly want. Why risk it all?"

And then we remember the stories we've heard time and again about leaders who've made bad choices that cost them everything.

And *then* we think of the temptations we have faced ourselves.

The words, "Everybody has their price," echo in my mind from a doctoral course I took with Professor Dr. Arch Hart of Fuller Theological Seminary. He had just told several stories of individuals who had fallen into temptation, in the process sacrificing their positions, reputations, and prestige for which they had worked their lifetimes to achieve. Then he looked at us and said, "Everybody has their price. What's yours?"

Dr. Hart then gave us thirty minutes to find a place where we could be alone and reflect on our response. It was a soul-searching time, to say the least.

I suggest you delve deeper into the account of King Asa, whose religious reforms and trust in God, when faced with an overwhelming invasion of Ethiopians, were overshadowed by his unbelieving political alliance with pagan King Ben-Hadad of Aram (see 2 Chronicles 16:1-14).

Or King Hezekiah's prideful exhibition of his wealth following a lifetime of faithful rule that led to the loss of all those riches (see 2 Kings 20:12-19 and 2 Chronicles 32:24-26).

Or King Josiah's arrogant defiance of King Neco's warning to avoid interfering in Egypt's conflict with Babylon, which led to Josiah's untimely death, despite his great national reforms (see 2 Chronicles 35:20-27).

Rather than shake our heads in amazement, these accounts remind us that faithfulness is not a once-and-for-all event, but a daily choice. We must heed Paul's exhortation, "Now these things happened to them as an example, but they were written down for our instruction, on whom the end of the ages has come. Therefore, let anyone who thinks that he stands take heed lest he fall" (1 Corinthians 10:11-12, ESV).

We have no excuse for carelessness. We can never let down our guard and indulge in a "foolish whim" that we know conflicts with God's will.

As you would expect, however, God's grace is bigger than any and all human failings. Repentance never ceases to open the windows of heaven.

62
The Repentance Reset

Every time I read the story of King Manasseh, Hezekiah's wicked son, I never cease to be amazed at the depth of human sin—or at the length and breadth and height and depth of God's grace (see Romans 8:38-39).

Manasseh was born following Hezekiah's miraculous healing, a time when God added fifteen years to the king's life (see 2 Kings 20:1-6). Manasseh began to rule at age twelve after Hezekiah's death. We might have expected a child born in the aftermath of a divine healing to be especially sensitive to honoring God, but that was not true of Manasseh. The first nine verses describing his reign read like a catalog of sin and abomination. Consider just one short sample:

> And [Manasseh] burned his son as an offering and used fortune-telling and omens and dealt with mediums and with necromancers. He did much evil in the sight of the Lord, provoking him to anger (2 Kings 21:6, ESV).

The account of Manasseh's reign in the Book of Kings ends in utter darkness. But the author of the parallel account in the Book of Chronicles adds to his story in a way that we should never forget (and might never have expected).

Following God's declaration of judgment against Manasseh, this King of Judah was taken prisoner by Assyrian armies, who "captured Manasseh with hooks and bound him with chains of bronze and brought him to Babylon" (2 Chronicles 33:11, ESV). As we read, most of us probably think, *Good! He certainly deserved that after all his wickedness.*

But then the very next verses surprise us: "And when he was in distress, Manasseh entreated the favor of the Lord his God and humbled himself greatly before the God of his fathers. He prayed to him, and *God was moved by his entreaty and heard his plea and brought him again to Jerusalem into his kingdom. Then Manasseh knew that the Lord was God*" (2 Chronicles 33:12-13, ESV, emphasis added).

Read those verses again, slowly. Perhaps you react like me: "You've got to be kidding me!" I'm not proud of my reaction, but I am being absolutely candid.

I continually underestimate God's grace. I tend to think that, maybe I'm not *that* bad, and that I can understand God showing grace to me and others like me. But *Manasseh?* And others I wouldn't dare to name in print or out loud? Come on! *Seriously?*

Yes. Seriously.

Repentance resets our lives. Period. Start of story.

> I'm absolutely convinced that nothing—nothing living or dead, angelic or demonic, today or tomorrow, high or low, thinkable or unthinkable—absolutely nothing can get between us and God's love because of the way that Jesus our Master has embraced us (Romans 8:38-39, The Message).

I don't know where you are on your journey as a disciple or as a leader, but this I know for sure: if you want to be God's person, God's leader, God will welcome you into his family and into his service. If you have failed big time in your own eyes, know that it's not too big for God. *That's* what is so amazing about grace.

Theologian Paul Tillich struggled with a personal dark side. Many knew that he led a life of sexual infidelity and debauchery. He declared to his wife, Hannah, as he was nearing death: "My poor Hannachen, I was very base to you, forgive me."[172] Eugene Peterson wrote about his own response to these revelations about Tillich in his book, *The Wisdom of Each Other: A Conversation Between Spiritual Friends*. Initially, Peterson reveled in Tillich's fresh and energetic theology. But here's how he describes discovering Tillich's dark side:

> And then I found out that he [Tillich] was a compulsive philanderer and a dabbler in pornography. I stormed into the study of my pastor, striking a tragic pose, and said, "I'm totally disillusioned!" He slapped his hand on his desk and said, "Good! Who wants to go around stuck with a bunch of illusions! Jesus is not going to disillusion you."

> Initially, I was put off by his lack of sympathy but since then have appreciated his wisdom. He was right. We are in a fight for truth and God-reality—illusions are dangerous in this business. We need to know the human heart in this business. We need to know the human heart and the surrounding culture as they are, deceitfully wicked and infested with prowling lions.

The Christian life is not romantic. And it certainly doesn't assume the best in everyone—particularly preachers. In some ways we assume the worst, but without despair, for it is because of this "worst" that we are in the salvation business, not out selling religious cosmetics.[173]

In light of all this, it's fascinating to read what Tillich himself wrote about grace. It is one of the most powerful statements on grace I have ever encountered:

Grace strikes us when we are in great pain and restlessness. It strikes us when we walk through the dark valley of a meaningless and empty life. It strikes us when we feel that our separation is deeper than usual, because we have violated another life, a life which we loved, or from which we were estranged. It strikes us when our disgust for our own being, our indifference, our weakness, our hostility, our lack of direction and composure have become intolerable to us. It strikes us when year after year the longed-for perfection of life does not appear, when the old compulsions reign within us as they have for decades, when despair destroys all joy and courage. Sometimes at that moment a wave of light breaks into our darkness, and it is as though a voice were saying: "You are accepted. You are accepted, accepted by that which is greater than you, and the name of which you do not know. Do not ask for the name now; perhaps you will find it later. Do not try to do anything now; perhaps later you will do much. Do not seek for anything; do not perform anything; do not intend anything. Simply accept the fact that you are accepted!"[174]

Nobody should ever use Tillich's behavior, nor his theology of grace, as a rationale for sin. That would be an abomination. But embrace his message—and let the Lord pour Living Water into the deepening well of your soul. The words of 1 John come to mind:

My little children, I am writing these things to you so that you may not sin. But if anyone does sin, we have an advocate with the Father, Jesus Christ the righteous. He is the propitiation for our sins, and not for ours only but also for the sins of the whole world. And by this we know that we have come to know him, if we keep his commandments (1 John 2:1-3, ESV).

This is the repentance reset, a holy recalibration that renews our relationship with the Lord and sets us back on course. It's the whole purpose of Jesus' mission: to redeem us from death and to call us continually into the abundant life of love and obedience.

63
Make Your Choice

It's not enough to read about grace and leadership and discipline and feel good. It's time to decide.

Decisions and commitments energize our lives. They shape our future dramatically, whether for better or worse. "First we make our commitments, then our commitments make us."[175]

God's people in the Old Testament faced countless life-changing choices. The most dramatic one lengthened their time in the wilderness from less than two years to forty years. Geographically, the journey to the promised land was not long. The distance between Cairo and Jerusalem in today's terms is a mere 263 miles (423 kilometers).[176] Spiritually and militarily, however, the Israelites faced a much greater distance.

Spiritually, the Lord wanted to shape his people from the very outset. That is why he led them to Mount Sinai, where they vividly experienced the majesty and glory of God. There they received the Ten Commandments, along with the essence of God's moral and civil governance and the divine plans for constructing the tabernacle. The tabernacle was the most tangible expression of God's continuing presence in covenant grace with his people.

Militarily, scripture says the Lord did not lead the people via the most direct route, the way of the sea, because they were unprepared for battle at that level: "When Pharaoh let the people go, God did not lead them by way of the land of the Philistines, although that was near. For God said, 'Lest the people change their minds when they see war and return to Egypt.' But God led the people around by the way of the wilderness toward the Red Sea" (Exodus 13:17-18, ESV).

After the exodus and within approximately eleven months of walking in the Sinai wilderness, the Lord began to lead his people to the Promised Land, their ultimate destination (see Numbers 10:11). When they reached the border of Canaan, the Lord allowed them to send spies ahead to reconnoiter the land.[177] When the spies returned, however, they gave contradictory recommendations. While all agreed that the Lord's description of the land as "good" was accurate, only Joshua and Caleb believed that the Lord would give them victory over the giants in the land (see Numbers 13:32-33). Most of the spies insisted they could not win. Consequently, the community panicked and refused to proceed one step further. They chose to disobey God's command … and it cost them dearly:

> And the Lord said to Moses, "How long will this people despise me? And how long will they not believe in me, in spite of all the signs that I have done among them?…" Then the Lord said, "I have pardoned, according to your word. But truly, as I live, and as all the earth shall be filled with the glory of the Lord, none of the men who have seen my glory and my signs that I did in Egypt and in the wilderness, and yet have put me to the test these ten times and have not obeyed my voice, shall see the land that I swore to give to their fathers. And none of those who despised me shall see it… And your children shall be shepherds in the wilderness forty years and shall suffer for your faithlessness, until the last of your dead bodies lies in the wilderness. According to the number of the days in which you spied out the land, forty days, a year for each day, you shall bear your iniquity forty years, and you shall know my displeasure" (Numbers 14:11, 20-23, 33-34, ESV).

Wow! That's a serious judgment. A passage like this helps us better understand, "The fear of the Lord is the beginning of wisdom" (Proverbs 1:7, ESV). So, we all face an essential question: Whom or what will I fear more? Will I fear human beings (see Psalm 27:1-3) or threatening circumstances (see Psalm 46)? Or will I take refuge in my all-powerful, all-knowing, all-wise, all-gracious, Almighty God?

As you contemplate the giants that stalk the borders of your own future promised land, what choice will you make? What will that look like for you?

Joshua's declaration, a generation after the border rebellion, gives us a powerful model: "Choose this day whom you will serve, whether the gods your fathers served in the region beyond the River, or the gods of the Amorites in whose land you dwell. But as for me and my house, we will serve the Lord" (Joshua 24:15, ESV).

It's important to remember that Jesus offers us a moment-by-moment choice: "And he said to all, 'If anyone would come after me, let him deny himself and take up his cross daily and follow me'" Luke 9:23, ESV).

How would you describe the choice you face?

> Does your identity in Christ give you meaning in life?
> Does your destiny in Christ motivate you?
> Does your partnership in Christ shape your mindset in everything, every time, with everyone?
> Have you honestly wrestled with a season of carelessness?
> Do you need a repentance reset?

Do you face a choice to stop rowing? That's a choice to turn from being self-sufficient to being soul-sufficient, from being self-reliant to relying on the Lord—that is, letting the Holy Spirit fill your sails.

You may feel like you've wandered in the wilderness a long time. The good news is that God desires to shorten that time and lead you onward to the promised land He intends for you! And that can begin now. It's *not* too late. As one New Testament writer said,

> Exhort one another every day, as long as it is called "today," that none of you may be hardened by the deceitfulness of sin. For we have come to share in Christ, if indeed we hold our original confidence firm to the end. As it is said,

> "Today, if you hear his voice,
> do not harden your hearts as in the rebellion"
> (Hebrews 3:13-15, ESV).

The apostle Paul conveyed the same urgency:

> For he [the Lord] says,

> "In a favorable time I listened to you,
> and in a day of salvation I have helped you."

> Behold, now is the favorable time; behold, now is the day of salvation (2 Corinthians 6:2, ESV, quoting Isaiah 49:8).

God is more eager to work in you and through you than you can imagine. You don't have to work yourself up emotionally, nor do you have to undergo a formal process. It's as simple as saying a prayer and then starting a new journey with Jesus.

You may already have committed your life to Jesus Christ, but now you realize God wants so much more for you. Don't waste any time on regrets! Focus on what lies ahead. As Paul writes, "But one thing I do: forgetting what lies behind and straining forward to what lies ahead, I press on toward the goal for the prize of the upward call of God in Christ Jesus" (Philippians 3:13-14, ESV).

Press on! Allow the Lord to fill your sails and then take a journey to some amazing place you've not yet imagined.

64
Fill My Sails, Lord!

Pull in your oars and put up your sail!

You cannot succeed in your own strength. You may be very intelligent, but you are not smart enough for what God wants to do through you.

You may have a great many talents, but you are not gifted enough for what the Spirit wants to do through you.

You may have passion, but you can do nothing on your own to bring lasting change to any human heart, whether yours or someone else's.

It all depends on God. It's all up to God working in and through you, according to His will and power at work in you.

What Kind of Impact Will You Have?

All of us want to experience a significant, satisfying life.

Significance comes from doing something that produces a lasting impact. What kind of ultimate contribution would you like to make to the world? Such an impact can be measured in terms of lives improved, people growing, individuals coming to faith in Christ, customers experiencing quality products and services, students growing in knowledge and wisdom, and the like.

Satisfaction comes from doing your work well and savoring the fruit of your labors. That fruit can take a variety of forms. It might be the fruit of knowing that you chose the way of integrity, even though it cost you career advancement. It might be the fruit of overcoming a threat or challenge. It might be the fruit of discovering God's power and direction in the middle of chaos and confusion. It might be the fruit of financial well-being that allows you to support ministries around the corner and around the world.

Will You Put up Your Sail?

None of this will happen automatically!

You must make the intentional choice to shift from the pursuit of success to the pursuit of God's kingdom. Jesus says it best: "Seek the

Kingdom of God above all else, and live righteously, and he will give you everything you need" (Matthew 6:33, NLT).

Jesus died to make this type of life possible. He gave us the Holy Spirit to dwell within us. The Bible often pictures the Holy Spirit through images of energy—wind and water and fire. The Spirit is our Comforter, which might better be understood as our "come-fortifier." The Spirit comes to us with comfort when we struggle and offers us strength to overcome those struggles.

But the Spirit awaits your invitation! Many scriptures encourage you and me to surrender our lives to the Holy Spirit by opening our hearts to Him. One of the most important of these passages is found in Ephesians:

> So be careful how you live. Don't live like fools, but like those who are wise. Make the most of every opportunity in these evil days. Don't act thoughtlessly but understand what the Lord wants you to do. Don't be drunk with wine, because that will ruin your life. Instead, be filled with the Holy Spirit (Ephesians 5:15-18, NLT).

In this passage, Paul compares the filling of the Holy Spirit to being filled with wine. He has in mind one thing being "under the influence of" another thing. In our rowing-sailing analogy, the filling of the Holy Spirit is like the wind, drawing from an image Jesus used, "The wind blows where it wishes, and you hear its sound, but you do not know where it comes from or where it goes. So it is with everyone who is born of the Spirit" (John 3:8, ESV).

You receive the Holy Spirit when you believe in Jesus Christ (see Ephesians 1:13-14). You live in the power of the Holy Spirit, however, when you intentionally surrender control of your life to him. Like the child who learns to float on water through time and trust, you learn to float—or sail—by trusting the Spirit, moment by moment.

Not only do you trust in the Lord, but the Lord trusts in you. "You did not choose me," says Jesus, "but I chose you and appointed you so that you might go and bear fruit—fruit that will last—and so that whatever you ask in my name the Father will give you. This is my command: Love each other" (John 15:16-17, ESV).

This verse holds the key to lasting fruit: loving people. Not monuments, but relationships. How do you translate that into everyday life? It's how you do what you do. It's about framing what you do in terms of helping others lead a good life, an honorable life, a grateful life.

I urge you to live each day in light of your eternal destiny. "Therefore, my dear brothers and sisters, stand firm. Let nothing move you. Always give yourselves fully to the work of the Lord, because you know that your labor in the Lord is not in vain" (1 Corinthians 15:58, NLT).

First Corinthians 15 is one of the most important passages in Paul's writings on the authenticity of Jesus' resurrection and its stupendous implications. In light of the resurrection and the certainty of eternal life, you might have expected Paul to write, "Don't worry so much about what you do in this world. Eternity's waiting!" But Paul clearly gave the opposite message: "Eternity's ahead, so pay attention to what you do here—and how you do it—because it has eternal implications!"

Pull in your oars and put up a sail! The Lord is about to take you on a journey you've always longed for but never thought possible. May you experience the most significant and satisfying life ever in Christ.

Amen and amen!

Acknowledgments

This book is the second primary product in the Lorica Ministries repertoire of *SoulShaping®* Resources. We continue to pursue our passion of equipping business leaders, pastors, congregations, and organizations to experience spiritual health and vitality in Christ through practical resources and dynamic support in spiritual coaching and mentoring.

Special thanks to The McAlpine Family Foundation for the vision and primary funding to bring this dream to reality. And thanks to the many supporters who provide prayer and financial support for this ministry.

I also want to express my abundant gratitude:

To my editor, Steve Halliday. Steve brings not only his skills as an editor for some of the finest authors today, but also the mind and heart of a pastor. I am honored to have him as part of my team—I hope for many more projects.

To Gail Herrmann, my copy editor.

To our daughter-in-love, Katie King Rumford, who formatted this manuscript for publication and also designed both the cover and the sketches for the five parts of this book.

To the board of Lorica Ministries, a not-for-profit ministry, comprised of John McAlpine, Jeff Herrmann, and Bill Hoyt. I'm humbled by your support and excited about the vision the Lord has given us to equip individuals, leaders, and congregations to experience spiritual vitality and intentional living through practical resources and dynamic support in spiritual coaching and mentoring.

And, saving the best for last, to my amazing partner in life and ministry, special thanks to my wife Sarah, and our family. The Lord has blessed me beyond measure with your love, wisdom, and support.

Endnotes

Introduction

1   *The Confessions of St. Augustine*, translated by Rex Warner, (New York: New American Library, 1963), specifically from Book 1, Chapter 1, Section 1, 17.

2   I remember first hearing the phrase, "Pull in your oars and put up a sail," from Father Terry Fulham, Episcopal priest at St. Paul's Church, Darien, Connecticut in the early 1980s.

3   Douglas J. Rumford, *SoulShaping (Second Edition): From Soul Neglect to Spiritual Vitality*, (Orange, CA: Lorica Ministries, 2022), 2.

4   The phrase "inner game" was popularized by W. Timothy Gallwey, *The Inner Game of Tennis: The Classic Guide to the Mental Side of Peak Performance*, Random House Publishing Group, 1977.

5   Robert J. Anderson and William A. Adams, *Mastering Leadership: An Integrated Framework for Breakthrough Performance and Extraordinary Results*, (Hoboken, NJ: John Wiley & Sons, Inc. 2016). 29.

6   C. S. Lewis, *The Letters of C. S. Lewis to Arthur Greeves*, (30 May 1916), par. 7, p. 104. Cited in Wayne Martindale and Jerry Root, Editors, *The Quotable Lewis*, (Wheaton: IL, Tyndale House Publishers, Inc. 1990), 622, #1553.

Part One What's Soul Got to Do with It?

7   John Keats, "Letter to George and Georgiana Keats (Feb. 14-May 3, 1819," in *The Norton Anthology of English Literature: Revised*, (New York, W. W. Norton & Company, 1968), 580.

8   J. Oswald Sanders, *Spiritual Leadership*, (Chicago: Moody Press, 1967). 13-14.

Chapter 1 Going for the Gold

9   *Turteltaub, Jon*, director. *Cool Runnings*. Burbank, CA: Walt Disney Pictures, 1993. Film. For further research, see Stokes, Nelson Christian. *Cool Runnings and Beyond: The Story of the Jamaica Bobsleigh Team*. Edited by Jim Cotton. Illustrated by John Wik. Salt Lake City, UT: American Book Publishing Group, 2002.

Chapter 2 Something's Missing

10   Arthur C. Brooks, *From Strength to Strength: Finding Success, Happiness, and Deep Purpose in the Second Half of Life* (New York: Portfolio, 2022), xiv.

11   Brooks, *Strength to Strength*, xiii.

12   Bob Buford, *Halftime: Moving from Success to Significance* (Grand Rapids, MI: Zondervan, 2015), 83.

13   https://www.azlyrics.com/lyrics/rollingstones/icantgetnosatisfaction.html, accessed on June 2, 2025.

14   Bob Buford, *Halftime: Moving from Success to Significance*, 19-20.

Chapter 3 What's Missing?

15 Lee G. Bolman and Terrence E. Deal, *Leading with Soul: An Uncommon Journey of Spirit*, Jossey-Bass, 1995), 169 [Cited from S. Mitchell (ed.), The Enlightened Mind: An Anthology of Sacred Prose (New York: HarperCollins, 1991), 191].

16 Ernest J. Lewis "Goodbye God—I'm Going to College" Unpublished sermon, p. 4-5 delivered at College Hill Presbyterian Church, Cincinnati, Ohio, no date.

17 Tilden Edwards, *Living Simply Through the Day: Spiritual Survival in a Complex Age*, (Paulist Press: New York, N.Y. 1977), 152.

18 Grok, artificial intelligence developed by xAI, response to query on Blaise Pascal's Pensées, August 16, 2025.

19 Adapted from Timothy Keller, *Center Church: Doing Balanced, Gospel-Centered Ministry in Your City* (Grand Rapids, MI: Zondervan, 2012), 127.

20 Charles Colson and Nancy Pearcey, *How Now Shall We Live*, (Wheaton: IL, Tyndale House Publishers, 1999), 14.

Chapter 4 You Gotta Have Soul

21 Douglas J. Rumford, *SoulShaping (Second Edition)*, Adapted from Appendix C.

22 Dallas Willard, *Personal Soul Care*, "The Soul and The Great Commandment," published on the website www.dwillard.org, accessed on June 2, 2025.

Chapter 5 A Metaphor for Satisfaction, Significance, and Joy

23 This a favorite phrase of Presbyterians, based on 1 Corinthians 14:40, "Let all things be done decently and in order," (King James Version).

Chapter 6 From Compartmentalization to Integration

24 Douglas J. Rumford, *SoulShaping (Second Edition)*, 229.

Chapter 7 The Inner Game Runs the Outer Game

25 W. Timothy Gallwey, *The Inner Game of Tennis: The Classic Guide to the Mental Side of Peak Performance*, (Random House Publishing Group, 1977), 11.

26 Anderson and Adams, *Mastering Leadership*, 27.

27 Derek Kidner, *Proverbs: Tyndale Old Testament Commentaries*, (Downers Grove, IL: Inter-Varsity Press, 1964), 68.

Chapter 9 Sink, Don't Skim

28 Adam Neder, *Theology as a Way of Life* (Grand Rapids, Michigan: Baker Academic, 2019), 128.

29 Nouwen, Henri J.M., Donald P. McNeill, and Douglas A. Morrison, *Compassion: A Reflection on the Christian Life* (Garden City, NY: Doubleday, 1982), 20, 21.

30 C. S. Lewis, *The Weight of Glory* (Grand Rapids, Michigan: William B. Eerdmans Publishing Company, 1949), 14-15.

Chapter 10 Scarboy

31 David and Karen Mains, *Tales of the Resistance* (Elgin, IL: Chariot Books, David C. Cook Publishers, 1986), pp. 37-41.

Chapter 11 Start with Who Before Why

32   Sinek, Simon, *Start with Why: How Great Leaders Inspire Everyone to Take Action.* (London: Penguin Books, 2011).

Chapter 12 Who Tells You Who You Are?

33   Studs Terkel, *American Dream: Lost & Found* (New York: Pantheon Books, 1980), page not available.

Chapter 13 The World Says, "You Are What You DO"

34   Tim Hansel, *When I Relax, I Feel Guilty*, (Elgin, IL: David C. Cook, 1979), 12.
35   Fenelon, *Let Go*, (Whitaker House, 1973), Letters 11 and 13.
36   Richard Kriegbaum, *Leadership Prayers* (Wheaton, IL: Tyndale House Publishers, 1980), 4.
37   Richard Kriegbaum, *Leadership Prayers*, 3, emphasis added.

Chapter 14 The World Says, "You Are What You OWN"

38   The exception, of course, is for those who take religious vows obligating themselves to an ascetic lifestyle, usually characterized by poverty, chastity, and obedience.
39   C. S. Lewis, *Mere Christianity*, (New York: Collier Books Macmillan Publishing Company, 1952), Book III, Chap. 3, 81-82.

Chapter 15 The World Says, "You Are Who You KNOW"

40   https://dougrumford.com/2017/10/02/gilt-by-association/ Posted on October 2, 2017.

Chapter 16 The World Says, "You Are Your POSITION"

41   Matthew A. Elliott, *Faithful Feelings, Rethinking Emotion in the New Testament* (Grand Rapids: Kregel, 2006), 194.
42   Matthew A. Elliott, *Faithful Feelings, Rethinking Emotion in the New Testament*, 194.
43   https://appleseeds.org/indispen-man_saxon.htm, Copyright 1959. "The Indispensable Man" was originally published in "The Nutmegger Poetry Club under the pen name Saxon Uberuaga. Saxon White Kessinger is her real name.
44   https://www.artofmanliness.com/character/advice/there-is-no-indispensable-man/.

Chapter 17 Identity Is Received, Not Achieved

45   Henri Nouwen, *Compassion: A Reflection in the Christian Life* (McNeill, Morrison), 20, 21.
46   https://poets.org/poem/gods-grandeur, accessed June 24, 2025.
47   https://www.youtube.com/watch?v=vpEaCp8iiSc, accessed June 24, 2025.
48   Ethel May Baldwin and David Benson, *Henrietta Mears and how she did it!* (Glendale, California: Gospel Light Regal Books, 1966), 17.
49   Douglas J. Rumford, "How to Say No Graciously" Leadership Journal, Fall, 1982, 94.
50   Perfection seems to be a righteous expectation. If we return to the Sermon on the Mount, Jesus says, "Be perfect, therefore, as your heavenly Father is perfect" (5:48). Jesus seems to be saying that we should never have a moral failure. A careful study of this passage, however, reveals a different intent behind Jesus' words. He is not requiring us to be morally faultless. The Greek word translated as 'perfect' is *teleios*. "You must be *teleios* as your heavenly Father is *teleios*." *Teleios* means "the goal, the consummation, the final purpose toward" which we are moving. It originally meant

"the turning point, hinge, the culminating point at which one stage ends and another begins." From this, it came to mean "maturing," or being at the proper stage at the proper time. This nuance of meaning helps us understand that the journey, not just the arrival at the goal, is what matters to God. As such it means fulfilling the intended purpose for a particular stage in development. The concern is not that we've arrived, but that we continue to face and travel in the right direction. In the central valley of California, for example, you can drive the Blossom Trail in springtime, when all the trees are in full bloom. It is a glorious, fragrant ride. As you drive along the Blossom Trail, you could say, "Those trees are *teleios*; those trees are perfect." They are right where they are supposed to be at this season, at this time in their life stage. Granted, mature fruit is not yet on the trees, but the conditions are right at that stage of blossoming for fruit to be produced, in time. If you drove the Blossom Trail in the summer, you would see the fruit just beginning to take shape. It hasn't ripened yet, but you could still say, "That is *teleios* fruit." Why? It's not ripe yet, but it's perfect for the season. This explanation is excerpted from Douglas J. Rumford *SoulShaping: Taking Care of Your Spiritual Life*, (First Edition) (Wheaton, IL: Tyndale House Publishers, 1996), 410-420.

Chapter 19 Partners in God's Continuing Work

51   Dale Bruner, *Matthew: A Commentary, Volume 1: The Christbook* (Grand Rapids, Michigan, William B. Eerdman Publishing Company, 2004), 188.

52   James S. Hewett, *Illustrations Unlimited* (Wheaton, IL: Tyndale House Publishers, 1988), 292.

Chapter 20 Identity Sets Healthy Boundaries

53   Edwin H. Friedman, *Generation to Generation: Family Process in Church and Synagogue* (New York: The Guilford Press, 1985), 27.

54   Dr. Henry Cloud and Dr, John Townsend, *Boundaries: When to Say Yes, When to Say No to Take Control of Your Life* (Grand Rapids, Michigan: Zondervan Publishing House, 1992), 25, 29.

55   Nora Sabahat Takieddine, SEP, EMDR Trained, www.GoodTherapy.org. Accessed June 26, 2025.

Chapter 21 Who Is a Leader?

56   Much of this material is adapted from Douglas J. Rumford, "Preface," *TouchPoints for Leaders: God's Wisdom for Leading in Work, Life, and Ministry* (Carol Stream, IL: Tyndale House Publishers, 2004), v-vi.

57   Warren Bennis and Burt Nanus, *Leaders: The Strategies for Taking Charge*, (New York: Harper & Row Publishers, 1985), 4.

58   Charles Hodge (1797-1878), American Presbyterian theologian and principal of Princeton Theological Seminary between 1851 and 1878. This quote is from Charles Hodge, *Romans* commentary. No additional citation available.

59   EQ refers to a person's emotional intelligence. Daniel Goleman writes, "It's not your IQ; it's how you manage yourself and your relationships." https://danielgolemanemotionalintelligence.com/ei-overview-the-four-domains-and-twelve-competencies/, Accessed June 26, 2025.

60   As far as I know, this concept is original with me. I have not yet developed an assessment to determine SQ.

61   Bobby Clinton, Table C-1 Research Papers Dealing with Finishing Well. https://bobbyclinton.com/articles/downloads/3FinishWellArticles.pdf, Accessed June 26, 2025.

62   The origin of the term "rest on your laurels" can be tracked back to ancient Greece. The expression referred to participants who had just completed their part of an athletic challenge, pausing to "rest" on their laurel wreath. Adapted from https://english-grammar-lessons.com/resting-on-your-laurels-meaning/, Accessed June 26, 2025.

63   Summary of Daniel Goleman's course found at https://danielgolemanemotionalintelligence.com/, Accessed June 26, 2025.

64   Mike Breen, *Building a Discipling Culture* (3DM Publishing, 2016), 42-48.

Chapter 22 Your Identity Will Be Tested

65   Breen, *Building a Discipling Culture*, 43.

66   *John Harvard's Journal*, 61, July-August 1982.

Chapter 24 Retirement Does Not Change Your Identity

67   Arthur Brooks, *From Strength to Strength*, 101.

68   For additional information on Lorica Ministries, please visit our website www.loricaministries.org

Chapter 26 Spiritual Disciplines Keep Your Inner Game of Identity Alive

69   These are disciplines are explained in Douglas Rumford, *SoulShaping (Second Edition)*, 130-167.

70   These are disciplines are explained in Douglas Rumford, *SoulShaping (Second Edition)*, 168-200.

Part Three Destiny: Pursue Your Ultimate Purpose

71   *Mr. Holland's Opus*, directed by Stephen Herek (1995; Hollywood Pictures).

Chapter 27 Futility Is Real in This Fallen World

72   Michael A. Eaton, *Ecclesiastes in Tyndale Old Testament Commentaries* series, (Downers Grove, IL: Inter-Varsity Press, 1983), 56.

Chapter 28 A Sense of Destiny

73   John Irving, *A Prayer for Owen Meany* (New York: William Morrow and Company). 1989.

74   I developed this summary from my own reading of the book as well as from https://www.sparknotes.com/lit/owenmeany/summary/, Accessed February 10, 2025. The 1998 movie *Simon Birch* is loosely based on this novel.

75   "The Sweet By-and-By" is a Christian hymn with lyrics by S. Fillmore Bennett.

Chapter 29 The Foundation for Our Motivation in Life

76   Douglas Rumford, *SoulShaping (Second Edition)*, 7-8.

Chapter 30 The Continuing Incarnation

77   https://en.wikipedia.org/wiki/Young_Life, Accessed June 11, 2025.

78   In today's missiological conversation, Jesus demonstrated the missional strategy of going out to people in contrast to the attractional strategy that expects others to come to us. It should also be noted that Jesus' incarnation included aspects that have nothing to do with us and our nature. Theologians speak of the ontological dimensions of Jesus being fully God and fully human, which were unique to his nature.

79   Rebecca Manley Pippert, *Out of the Saltshaker and into the World*. (Downers Grove, IL: InterVarsity Press, 1978), 177, 178.

Chapter 31 Living in Exile: Be Heavenly-Minded and Earthly Good

80   Christians designated the main epochs of history as BC, meaning "Before Christ" and AD, meaning *Anno Domini* the Latin abbreviation for 'in the year of our Lord (not "After Death"). It is now more common to use the designations BCE, meaning "Before the Common Era," and CE meaning "Common Era," but it's also appropriate to maintain BC and AD.

81   John Rinehart, *Gospel Patrons: People Whose Generosity Changed the World* (Reclaimed Publishing, 2018), 13.

82   See Chapter 55, "What Could God Do Through You?"

Chapter 32 What's the Real Bottom Line?

83   https://psychology-spot.com/memento-mori-meaning-origin/, Accessed June 17, 2025.

84   James A. K. Smith, *How (Not) to Be Secular* (Grand Rapids, MI: Wm. B. Eerdmans Publishing Co., 2014), viii.

85   Rodney Stark, *The Triumph of Christianity: How the Jesus Movement Became the World's Largest Religion* (San Francisco: HarperOne, 2011), 369.

Chapter 33 Our Perspective on Life Matters Ultimately

86   Elisabeth Elliot, *Through Gates of Splendor* (Wheaton, IL: Tyndale, 1981); also *Shadow of the Almighty* (San Francisco: HarperCollins, 1989).

Chapter 34 Rooted in Our Identity, Focused on Our Destiny

87   http://www.makefunoflife.net/everyday-inspiration/present-tense-by-jason-lehman, Accessed May 1, 2025.

Chapter 35 Get a Life? Or Shape a Life?

88   Douglas Rumford, *SoulShaping (Second Edition)*, 2.
89   Charles Dickens, *A Christmas Carol* (New York: Barnes & Noble Books, 1994), 102.
90   Douglas J. Rumford, *What About Heaven and Hell* (Wheaton, IL: Tyndale House Publishers, 2000), 39-61, gives a full treatment of my theology of judgment.

Chapter 36 Discover Your Personal Destiny by Paying Attention

91   https://bobbyclinton.com/downloads/articles/FocusedLife.pdf, Accessed June 17, 2025.
92   Douglas J. Rumford, *SoulShaping (Second Edition)*, 231.
93   https://bobbyclinton.com/downloads/articles/FocusedLife.pdf, Accessed June 17, 2025.
94   Douglas J. Rumford, *SoulShaping (Second Edition)*, 232-234.
95   Douglas J. Rumford, *SoulShaping (Second Edition)*, 237.

Chapter 37 Sail Consistently into Your Destiny

96   C.S. Lewis, "The Weight of Glory" in *The Weight of Glory and Other Addresses* (Grand Rapids, Michigan: Williams B. Eerdmans Publishing Company, 1949), 1-2.
97   Dallas Willard, *The Divine Conspiracy: Rediscovering Our Hidden Life in God* (HarperSanFranscisco, 1998), 283.
98   Douglas J. Rumford, *SoulShaping (Second Edition)*, 257.

99   Thomas Kelly, *A Testament of Devotion* (New York: Harper & Row Publishers, 1941), 39, 60, 61.

Chapter 38 Spiritual Disciplines Keep Your Inner Game of Destiny Alive

100   Randy Frazee and Max Lucado. *The Story: The Bible as One Continuing Story of God and His People* (Grand Rapids, MI: Zondervan, 2011).

101   Douglas J. Rumford, *SoulShaping (Second Edition)*, 80.

102   Douglas J. Rumford, *SoulShaping (Second Edition)*, 72-82.

103   Abraham Joshua Heschel, *The Sabbath: Its Meaning for Modern Man*, (New York: Farrar, Straus and Giroux, 1951 renewed 2005).

104   Heschel, *The Sabbath*, 13.

105   Heschel, *The Sabbath*, 10.

106   Douglas J. Rumford, *SoulShaping (Second Edition)*, 82, provides a summary of "Guidelines for Enjoying Sabbath Rest."

107   The background story for Preview is in *SoulShaping (Second Edition)*, pages 97-99. See more on this in Chapter 53.

108   Douglas J. Rumford, *SoulShaping (Second Edition)*, 104, provides a summary of my "Guidelines for The Discipline of Preview."

109   Douglas J. Rumford, *SoulShaping (Second Edition)*, 107.

110   Morning Prayer from *The Book of Common Prayer* http://justus.anglican.org/~ss/commonworship/word/morningbcp.html, Accessed June 20, 2025.

111   Another way to say this is that it's possible you may mistake your passionate desire for your destiny—but fulfill your ultimate destiny almost accidentally. That's not ideal, but it can happen.

112   See quote on page 112

Part Four Partnership: Link with God's Kingdom Agenda

113   A.W. Tozer, *The Pursuit of God*, (Wheaton, IL: Tyndale Houe Publishers, 1948) p. 127

114   George MacDonald, *Unspoken Sermons, Series 3*, (London: Longmans, Green, and Co. 1889).

115   A.W. Tozer, *The Pursuit of God*, p. 127. This is my paraphrase. Here's Tozer's actual quote: "The 'layman' need never think of his humbler task as being inferior to that of his minister. Let every man abide in the calling wherein he is called & his work will be as sacred as the work of the ministry. It is not what a man does that determines whether his work is sacred or secular, it is why he does it. The motive is everything. Let a man sanctify the Lord God in his heart & he can thereafter do no common act. All he does is good & acceptable to God thru Jesus Christ. For such a man, living itself will be sacramental & the whole world a sanctuary."

116   C. S. Lewis, *Mere Christianity*, 45-46.

Chapter 39 Do Everything Differently

117   Scott McCartney Wall Street Journal, *To a United Pilot, The Friendly Skies Are a Point of Pride. Capt. Flanagan Goes to Bat For His Harried Passengers; Still, Some Online Skeptics*, Aug. 28, 2007, https://www.wsj.com/articles/SB118826634834410559, Accessed on May 18, 2025. Quoted in sermon by Dr. Victor D. Pentz, Senior Pastor Peachtree Presbyterian Church, *You're Already There* in "My 95" sermon series.

Chapter 40 Leaders Are God's Partners in Kingdom Work

118   C. H. Dodd, *The Parables of the Kingdom*, rev. ed. (New York: Charles Scribner's Sons,

1961), 3. Quoted in David K. Naugle, *Reordered Love, Reordered Lives: Learning the Deep Meaning of Happiness*, (Grand Rapids, MI: William B. Eerdmans Publishing Company, 2008), 101.

119   George Ladd, *A Theology of the New Testament* (Grand Rapids, MI: Eerdmans, 1974), 48. Quoted by John Wimber with Kevin Springer, *Power Evangelism* (San Francisco: Harper Publishers 1986), 20, 21.

120   John Wimber with Kevin Springer, *Power Evangelism* (San Francisco: Harper Publishers, 1986), 21.

Chapter 41 Ministry in the Marketplace

121   I have been introducing myself this way for a long time, but I have since become aware that other pastors have also used this approach—and communicated their style through social media. Another evidence that there is nothing new under the sun!

122   Frank R. Tillapaugh, *Unleashing the Church: Getting People Out of the Fortress and into Ministry* (Ventura, CA: Regal Books, 1982), 19.

Chapter 42 Daniel: God's Servant in a Pagan Government

123   Daniel lived in Babylon from his captivity around 605 BC until the fall of Babylon in 539/538 BC, when Cyrus the Persian became ruler. Even then, Daniel continued to serve briefly under Cyrus, see Daniel 6:28.

Chapter 43 Holy Saboteurs

124   C. S. Lewis, *Mere Christianity*, 45-46.

125   Mark Gibbs & T. Ralph Morton, *God's Frozen People* (London: Fontana Books, 1964), 139.

Chapter 44 We're Not Just Passing Through

126   See Chapter 31, "Living In Exile."

127   The Lord provided a fascinating reason for the seventy years: "…to fulfill the word of the Lord by the mouth of Jeremiah, until the land had enjoyed its Sabbaths. All the days that it lay desolate it kept Sabbath, to fulfill seventy years" (2 Chronicles 36:21).

128   In the Islamic context, the goal of Shari'a law is to apply the divine will and law to every aspect of civic (political) and personal life. This contrasts with the Christian understanding that the comprehensive standards and expectations of faith *cannot* be imposed on those who do not believe. We do believe, of course, in the rule of moral law as expressed in the commandments against killing, stealing, lying, committing adultery, and so on. But Christians do not believe governments are responsible to compel people to worship, to tithe to the church, or to live by the requirements of a disciple.

129   I mentioned Vic Pentz in Chapter 39.

130   https://actoneprogram.com/about/, Accessed July 2, 2025.

131   Emailed to me on October 18, 2010, by Lesley S. and shared with her permission.

132   This is from my personal notes. While the benediction appears in numerous blogs, devotionals, and church resources no single book or sermon by Halverson is definitively cited as its first written appearance.

Chapter 46 Embrace Your Biblical Identity in the Workplace

133   My editor, Steve, shared the idea that it can be helpful to focus on being a "witness" rather than doing "evangelism." As far as I know, the word "evangelist" appears just

three times in the NT (Acts 21:8; Eph. 4:11; 2 Tim 4:5) and the word "evangelism" doesn't appear at all. The first mentions "Philip the evangelist," the second talks about God giving us the gift of evangelists (along with apostles, prophets, pastors, teachers, etc.), and the third tells Timothy, a pastor, to "do the work of an evangelist." To be a witness to God's work in your life seems much less intimidating than to do evangelism. Witnessing seems like a much broader and less specific activity, and it also seems more "natural" and less daunting.

134   Much later than my experience reported here, I read about this topic of candor in Ed Catmull's *Creativity, Inc: Overcoming the Unseen Forces that Stand in the Way of True Inspiration* (New York: Random House, 2014). The book tells the story of the first several years of Pixar. Chapter 5 is called "Honesty and Candor."

Chapter 47 Motives

135   Dennis Prager, *The Rational Bible: Genesis* (Washington, DC: Regnery Faith, 2019), 85-86.

136   Quoted in Jay Pathak & Dave Runyon, *The Art of Neighboring* (Grand Rapids, Michigan: Baker Books, 2012), 101-102.

137   Of course, we must acknowledge Paul's attitude when he wrote, "Some indeed preach Christ from envy and rivalry, but others from good will. The latter do it out of love, knowing that I am put here for the defense of the gospel. The former proclaim Christ out of selfish ambition, not sincerely but thinking to afflict me in my imprisonment. What then? Only that in every way, whether in pretense or in truth, Christ is proclaimed, and in that I rejoice" (Philippians 1:15-18, ESV). But it is still a matter for personal repentance when we discover this in ourselves.

Chapter 49 Confidence and Inadequacy

138   The term "Imposter Syndrome" was coined by psychologists Pauline Rose Clance and Suzanne Imes, first mentioned in their 1978 article, "The Impostor Phenomenon in High Achieving Women: Dynamics and Therapeutic Intervention," published in the journal *Psychotherapy: Theory, Research & Practice*. https://grok.com/chat/0f23f669-0ba2-4199-beb2-c3096ca5c539, Accessed on July 10, 2025.

139   https://grok.com/chat/4f419bc1-4619-4181-ab28-601980b3434a.

Chapter 50 Competing Values and Matters of Conscience

140   Douglas J. Rumford, *SoulShaping (Second Edition)*, 156-167.

141   Laura L. Nash, *Believers in Business* (Nashville: Thomas Nelson, 1994), Table of Contents, 37.

142   Mark Gibbs & T. Ralph Morton, *God's Frozen People*, 71.

143   Mark Gibbs & T. Ralph Morton, *God's Frozen People*, 71.

144   Charles H. Spurgeon, quoted in Doberstein, *Minister's Prayer Book* (Philadelphia, PA: Fortress Press, 1986), 226-227.

Chapter 51 Realize It or Not, You Are a Witness

145   We explored this concept briefly in Chapter 32 but develop a different aspect of it in this chapter.

146   James K. A. Smith, *How (Not) to Be Secular* (Grand Rapids, MI: Wm. B. Eerdmans Publishing Co., 2014), viii.

147   James K. A. Smith, *How (Not) to Be Secular*, vii-viii, emphasis added.

148   Emmanuel Célestin Suhard. *Priests Among Men*, cited by L'Engle, Madeleine, *Walking on Water: Reflections on Faith and Art* (Convergent Books, 2016), 29.

149   From my personal notes.

Chapter 52 A Rowing Partnership or a Sailing Partnership?

150   William Barclay, *The Letter to The Romans* (Philadelphia, PA, Westminster Press, 1955), 243.

Chapter 53 Spiritual Disciplines Keep Your Inner Game of Partnership Alive

151   Douglas J. Rumford, *SoulShaping (Second Edition)*, 94-104.
152   Douglas J. Rumford, *SoulShaping (Second Edition)*, chap. 18, 19, 20.
153   Douglas J. Rumford, *SoulShaping (Second Edition)*, 227-228.
154   See Chapter 36 "Discover Your Personal Destiny by Paying Attention."
155   Robert D. Putnam, *Bowling Alone* (New York: Simon & Schuster Paperbacks, 2000), 19.
156   Robert D. Putnam, *Bowling Alone*, 27, 28.

Part Five Fill My Sails, Lord

157   Mack R. Douglas, "Exactly Where Are You Going?" in *The Marriage Affair: The Family Counselor*, edited by J. Allan Petersen (Wheaton, IL: Tyndale House Publishers, 1971), 61.

158   Richard Rohr, *Falling Upward: A Spirituality for the Two Halves of Life* (San Francisco: Jossey-Bass, 2011), 201.

159   John Wesley, commonly attributed, in *The Oxford Dictionary of Quotations*, ed. Elizabeth Knowles, 5th ed. (Oxford: Oxford University Press, 1999), s.v. "John Wesley."

160   Source unknown. From my personal notes.

Chapter 55 What Could God Do Through You?

161   Michael Frost & Alan Hirsch, *The Shaping of Things to Come* (Peabody: Hendrickson Publishers, Inc., 2003), 104-105.

162   John Rinehart, *Gospel Patrons*. The following account is an adaptation and summary drawn from "The 18th-Century Revival," 61-89.

163   John Rinehart, *Gospel Patrons* p. 65.

164   John Rinehart, *Gospel Patrons* p. 71-72.

165   I have developed a small group resource called the "*SoulShaping* Experience for Small Groups" which provides videos and discussion guides to equip people to experience Christ's abundant life through spiritual vitality. For more information visit our Lorica Ministries website https://loricaministries.org/product/the-soulshaping-experience-kit-small-groups/.

Chapter 58 The Link Between Desire and Achievement

166   Douglas J. Rumford, *SoulShaping (Second Edition)*, 55.
167   Douglas J. Rumford, *SoulShaping (Second Edition)*, 72-82.
168   https://grok.com/chat/bea1e652-1952-48ce-b84b-408c0bd2f39c, Accessed July 14, 2025.

Chapter 59 Build Momentum

169   G. K. Chesterton, *What's Wrong with the World*, written in 1910. Part Four of the book is titled, "Education: Or the Mistake about the Child." The famous and much

abused line comes up at the end of Chapter 14 of that section. https://www.chesterton.org/a-thing-worth-doing/.

170   James Clear, *Atomic Habits*, (New York: Avery, 2018), 162.

171   James Clear, *Atomic Habits*, 164-165.

Chapter 62 The Repentance Reset

172   http://www.spirit-wars.com/html/paganspirituality.html accessed June 3, 2025.

173   John Mark Ministries website https://www.jmm.org.au/articles/9360.htm, Accessed on July 9, 2025, citing Eugene Peterson, *The Wisdom of Each Other: A Conversation Between Spiritual Friends* (Grand Rapids, MI: Zondervan, 1998), 47-48.

174   Paul Tillich, *The Shaking of the Foundations* (New York, Charles Scribner's Sons, 1948), 162.

Chapter 63 Make Your Choice

175   Douglas J. Rumford, *SoulShaping (Second Edition)*, 257.

176   https://duckduckgo.com/?q=distance+from+cairo+egypt+to+jerusalem+israel&atb=v478-1&ia=web, Accessed July 3, 2025.

177   The Bible offers two accounts of the spies. In Numbers 13:1-2 we read, "The Lord spoke to Moses, saying, 'Send men to spy out the land of Canaan, which I am giving to the people of Israel. From each tribe of their fathers you shall send a man, every one a chief among them.'" But in Deuteronomy 1:22-23, the idea for the spies seemed to originate with the people: "Then all of you came near me and said, 'Let us send men before us, that they may explore the land for us and bring us word again of the way by which we must go up and the cities into which we shall come.' The thing seemed good to me, and I took twelve men from you, one man from each tribe." This need not be seen as a contradiction. God could easily have permitted the people's request and then instructed Moses to proceed. Big problems emerged, however, with the people's response to the spies' reports.

About the Author

Douglas J. Rumford is a child of God through Jesus Christ who has served as an ordained Presbyterian pastor in churches for more than forty-four years. He is the founder and president of Lorica Ministries. Lorica Ministries empowers business leaders, pastors, congregations, and organizations to experience spiritual health and vitality in Christ through practical resources and dynamic support in spiritual coaching and mentoring.

In addition to *SoulShaping* (first and second editions) Doug has authored several books and Bible projects:

Scared to Life: Awakening the Courage of Faith in an Age of Fear, Wheaton, IL: Victor Books, 1994.

Questions God Asks, Questions Satan Asks, Wheaton, IL: Tyndale House Publishers, 1998.

What About Unanswered Prayer? Wheaton, IL: Tyndale House Publishers, 2000. (also translated and published in Korean by Word of Life Press, 2022)

What About Heaven and Hell? Wheaton, IL: Tyndale House Publishers, 2000.

What About Spiritual Warfare? Wheaton, IL: Tyndale House Publishers, 2000.

Doug developed and wrote the notes for *The Promise Bible*, *The Promise New Testament*, *TouchPoint Bible Promise*s, and *TouchPoints for Leaders*, all from Tyndale House Publishers.

SoulShaping® is a registered trademark.

Doug earned his Doctor of Ministry degree from Fuller Theological Seminary, Pasadena, California. He earned his Master of Divinity degree from Gordon-Conwell Theological Seminary, South Hamilton, Massachusetts, graduating summa cum laude as valedictorian. He earned a Bachelor of Arts in English from Miami University in Oxford, Ohio, graduating magna cum laude and Phi Beta Kappa.

Doug's blog, "Heart and Mind: A Spiritual Journal" can be found at www.dougrumford.com

For information and inquiries about Doug's resources, coaching and availability for speaking, visit the website www.loricaministries.org. Lorica Ministries is a not-for-profit ministry committed to empowering individuals, leaders, and congregations to experience spiritual vitality and intentional living through practical resources and dynamic support in curriculum, coaching, and consulting.

Doug and his wife, Sarah, live in Southern California and have four adult children and five grandchildren.

Doug's greatest joy is equipping people to experience Christ's abundant life through spiritual vitality and intentional living.

Shaping A Leader's Soul Workbook: A Personal Guide to Lasting Impact and Joyful Living

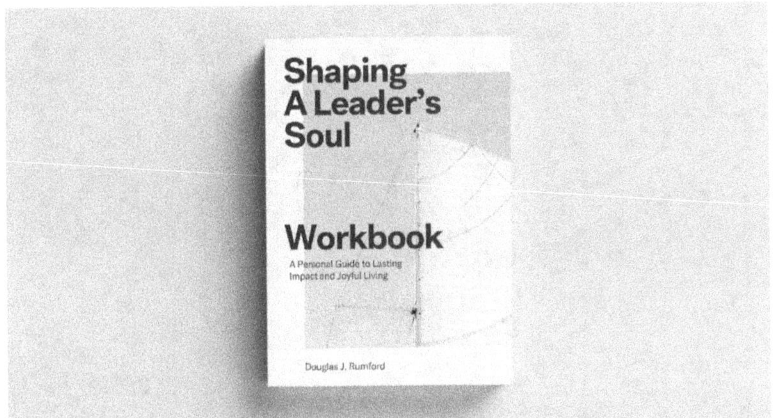

Shaping A Leader's Soul: For Lasting Impact and Joyful Living is a book that equips people with perspective, resilience, and spiritual vitality for living and leading in turbulent times. Competing values and diverse ideologies threaten the fabric of the social order from families to nations. At the most basic level, these are matters of the heart and soul.

The *Shaping A Leader's Soul Workbook: A Personal Guide to Lasting Impact and Joyful Living* expands on the themes of the book and helps translate ideas into practice. Framed as a ten-week overview of the book, the *Workbook* provides:

- questions for in-depth Bible study
- prompts for personal reflection
- assessments and exercises for personal and group engagement
- opportunities for practical planning and implementing ideas
- questions and ideas for group discussion

The *Shaping A Leader's Soul Workbook* provides the opportunity for a transforming experience that awakens and sustains spiritual vitality that reaches your head, your heart, and your life.

The *Shaping A Leader's Soul Workbook* is available in print and as an eBook.

SoulShaping (Second Edition): From Soul Neglect to Spiritual Vitality

SoulShaping (Second Edition): From Soul Neglect to Spiritual Vitality presents a readily accessible approach to the broad repertoire of spiritual disciplines that have nurtured God's people across the centuries.

Readers learn how to diagnose their spiritual condition using ten symptoms of soul neglect and then explore the strategies for spiritual change.

They are then introduced to the five vital signs of spiritual health and growth: God's pace redeems our time; God's presence fills our hearts; God's perspective renews our minds; God's power strengthens our wills; God's purpose directs our steps. Three specific spiritual disciplines support each vital sign.

SoulShaping concludes with practical guidance on how to develop a plan of soul-specific disciplines personally tailored to develop and maintain readers spiritual vitality.

SoulShaping (Second Edition): From Soul Neglect to Spiritual Vitality is available in print and as an eBook.

SoulShaping Journal:
Pathways to Spiritual Vitality

The *SoulShaping Journal: Pathways to Spiritual Vitality* is an additional resource to help readers translate information into genuine personal transformation. It highlights primary disciplines that form the foundation for spiritual vitality.

The *SoulShaping Journal: Pathways to Spiritual Vitality* provides input on how to keep a spiritual journal, along with exercises for daily reflection on Scriptures and the material in *SoulShaping*. Detailed steps guide readers through a ten-week process of developing their personal vision and soul plan.

The *SoulShaping Journal* is available in print and as an eBook.